SO-CGQ-024

Raisins & Dried Fruits

SERVING AMERICAN FAMILIES & THE WORLD SINCE 1912

SUN-MAID GROWERS OF CALIFORNIA
SUN-MAID CREATIVE TEAM
ANNA L. PALECEK
•
GARY H. MARSHBURN
•
BARRY F. KRIEBEL

13525 South Bethel Avenue
Kingsburg, CA 93631-9232
Tel: 1-559-896-8000
Email: smaid@sunmaid.com
Website: www.sunmaid.com

Special thanks to Jerry Winters, cover design
Copyright © 2011 Sun-Maid Growers of California

LONDON, NEW YORK, MUNICH,
MELBOURNE, DELHI

FOR DORLING KINDERSLEY: Managing Art Editor RICHARD CZAPNIK
Senior Editors MICHELE WELLS, ROS WALFORD • **Senior DTP Designer**
DAVID MCDONALD • **Production Editor** KAVITA VARMA • **Senior Production
Controller** SARAH HUGHES • **Associate Publisher** NIGEL DUFFIELD

First published in the United States in December 2011
by DK Publishing, 375 Hudson Street, New York, New York 10014

10 9 8 7 6 5 4 3 2 1
001-182142-Dec/11

Copyright Page Layout and Design © 2011 Dorling Kindersley Limited

DK books are available at special discounts when purchased in bulk for sales
promotions, premiums, fundraising, or educational use.

For details, contact: DK Publishing Special Markets, 375 Hudson Street,
New York, New York 10014. SpecialSales@dk.com

Library of Congress Cataloging-in-Publication Data
Palecek, Anna L., 1982-
  Sun-Maid Raisins & Dried Fruits : serving American families & the world since 1912
/ Sun-Maid Growers of California, Sun-Maid Creative Team, Anna L. Palecek, Gary H.
Marshburn, Barry F. Kriebel.
      p. cm.
  Version with recipes in imperial measurements.
  Summary: "A collection of over 50 recipes for raisins and dried fruits including the
story of their production from the field to the table"-- Provided by publisher.
  ISBN 978-0-7566-9067-0
  1. Cooking (Raisins) I. Marshburn, Gary H., 1952- II. Kriebel, Barry F., 1950- III.
Sun-Maid Growers of California. IV. Title.
  TX813.R34P35 2011
  641.4--dc23
                2011041399

ISBN: 978-0-7566-9067-0
Printed and bound in the U.S.A. by Worzalla

Discover more at
www.dk.com

SINCE 1912

SUN·MAID

Raisins & Dried Fruits

SERVING AMERICAN FAMILIES & THE WORLD SINCE 1912

Contents

CHAPTER 1
The
Basics

CHAPTER 2
The Background
Story

CHAPTER 3
The Sun-Maid
Story

Dedication

During Sun-Maid's first 100 years, millions of individuals contributed to Sun-Maid's success. Beginning in the late 1800s and continuing to this day, immigrants from many countries have developed California's Central Valley into one of the finest fruit and vegetable growing areas in the world. The region's unique combination of sun, soil, and water is ideal for producing quality sun-dried raisins and dried fruits. Hard work, tenacity, and vision drove early California raisin growers to succeed in carving out a legacy which has lasted for six generations. Annually, the families of Sun-Maid growers entrust their livelihoods to the Board of Directors, management, and employees of Sun-Maid to process and market each year's harvest to our valued customers in over 50 countries. Sun-Maid's success is dependent on a worldwide sales, logistics, and customer network, which assures that "every minute of the day, somewhere in the world, someone is eating Sun-Maid raisins." This publication is dedicated to all these individual efforts, combined contributions, and satisfied customers.

One very special note is to Kendall L. Manock, Sun-Maid's general counsel, who advised our Board and management from 1961 almost continuously until his death in 2010. Mr. Manock began his legal career as a United States Attorney, and as a clerk for the U.S. 9th Circuit Court of Appeals. With his partners, he developed a firm, which served the entire Fresno community well. For Sun-Maid, Mr. Manock was the ideal general counsel. He, like Sun-Maid, shared a national reputation for honesty, fairness, and reliability as a leader in the California agricultural community. For 50 years, Sun-Maid's growers and customers benefited from his sound legal and practical advice on the full range of challenging and ever changing commercial, legal, regulatory, and consumer issues. In many ways, Mr. Manock and Sun-Maid shared a deep kinship based on

serving the community interests of our producers and the national and international interests of our customers. In this sense, Mr. Manock's character typified that of the best customers, growers, employees, suppliers, and advisors who have been part of the Sun-Maid family. Mr. Manock passed away as we began in earnest the development of this publication. We hope that he and his family would be proud of it.

Kendall L. Manock
Sun-Maid General Counsel
1961 to 2010

Foreword

In celebration of our 100th Anniversary we are proud to release our publication *Sun-Maid: Raisins & Dried Fruits, Serving American Families & the World Since 1912.*

In developing this publication we made a conscious decision to focus on what we believe consumers and the public want to know today about Sun-Maid, and raisins and dried fruits, and to tell this story in a very visual way. In making this decision, we have sacrificed telling the complete story of so many key individuals.

These would have included H.H. Welsh and James Madison, our first Chairman and President, both elected in 1912; William N. Keeler, who served as President from 1931 to 1949; A.E. Swanson, our longest seated Chairman from 1944 to 1963; Pete J. Penner, our youngest Board member in history when first elected and who served tirelessly from 1968 to 2009, including as Chairman from 1986 to 1999; visionary growers Earl Rocca and sons and Lee Simpson, who could see the future for mechanical harvesting and overhead trellis systems for dried-on-the-vine crops, respectively, before others could; and key management and staff who successfully transitioned Sun-Maid into the 21st century. And of course, there were many, many more.

We tell the story of raisins and dried fruits from ancient times to today, how these are grown and harvested, what makes California a unique growing area, our links to consumers in over 50 countries, and how raisins and traditional dried fruits are equivalent to fresh fruit without the water. We include the story behind Lorraine Collett Petersen, whose likeness became our internationally recognized icon, the "Sun-Maid Girl," and E.A. Berg, our advertising manager, who in 1914 originated the name Sun-Maid and developed our first packaging and advertising campaigns.

We have included over 50 of the best raisin and dried fruit recipes in the world to help you and your families enjoy our products for celebrations or to make any day special. We especially thank those companies who granted Sun-Maid permission to use their recipes.

We hope that this publication exceeds your expectations. We welcome your comments at www.sunmaid.com.

Jon E. Marthedal
Chairman
Sun-Maid Growers of California

Barry F. Kriebel
President
Sun-Maid Growers of California

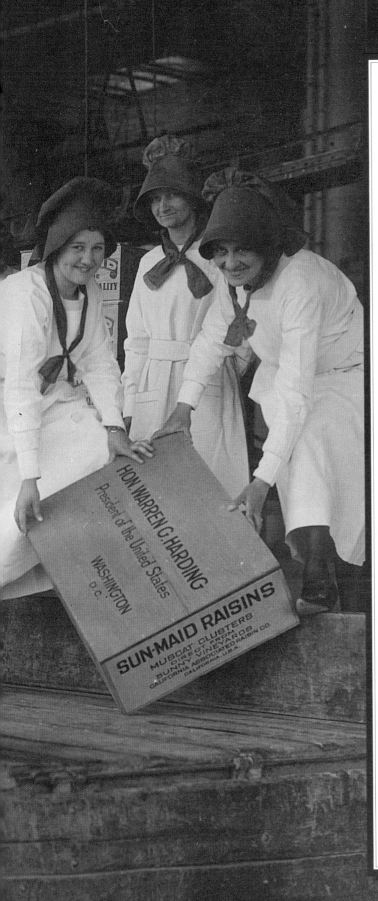

CHAPTER 1
The Basics

Sun-Maid Timeline 1900–1930

EARLY 1900s
The California raisin industry experiences tremendous growth in the fertile San Joaquin Valley.

1914
The new California Associated Raisin Company launches its first advertising program with a Raisin Train bound for Chicago. Placards on the cars proclaim: "Raisins Grown by 6,000 California Growers."

1900 1906—San Francisco earthquake   1914—World War I begins

1912
Fresno area San Joaquin Valley raisin growers propose a new grower-owned cooperative, the California Associated Raisin Company. H.H. Welsh is the Association's first chairman.

1914
Local advertising creative E.A. Berg originates the name "Sun-Maid." Besides referring to the fact that raisins are "made" in the California sun, the words suggested a personality—a pretty "maid" gathering the harvest and making the raisins.

1915
Sun-Maid participates in the Panama Pacific International Exposition held in San Francisco, demonstrating the raisin-seeding machine with Muscat raisins, providing raisin samples, passing out raisin bread, and giving away recipe books.

1915

The co-op adopts the name Sun-Maid. Sun-Maid director L.R. Payne sees Miss Lorraine Collett drying her hair in a red bonnet and asks her to pose for the painting, which would become the company's new trademark and soon one of America's most recognized brands.

1921

The Sun-Maid brand becomes a symbol of the San Joaquin Valley's agricultural economy and culture. The "sun maids" make many appearances promoting California raisins and the popular new brand, including hand-delivering Sun-Maid raisins to President Warren G. Harding along with an invitation to the annual Raisin Day festivities held in Fresno, California.

1923

The Sun-Maid Girl illustration is modified for the first time.

1918—World War I ends   **1929—Great Depression begins**   *1930*

1920s

Heavy planting of raisin vineyards causes overproduction and plummeting prices. Prohibition leads to a surplus of grapes that would have ordinarily been made into wine. The industry also struggles with serious financial problems brought on by the Great Depression.

1922

More than 85 percent of California raisin growers are members of the co-op, which changes its name to Sun-Maid Raisin Growers of California to identify more closely with its nationally recognized brand.

1918

The cooperative opens its new processing plant in Fresno, California, dubbed "the finest factory building this side of Detroit." It would be Sun-Maid's home from 1918–1964.

Sun-Maid Timeline 1930–1965

1926–1932
Renowned American artist Norman Rockwell creates the first of a number of paintings for use in Sun-Maid advertising.

1948
The Berlin Airlift brings supplies to the western section of Berlin blockaded by the Soviet Union. "Raisin Bomber" pilots collect raisins, candy, chocolate, and gum, and sew them into miniature parachutes dropped to children waiting by the airfields below.

U.S. BERLIN AIRLIFT

Americans to Fly Tons of Food Over Russian Blockade

Washington, D.C., July 1, 1948—The President annouced U.S. efforts to airlift food to needy Germans due to the Russian

1941–1945
World War II influences every aspect of American life. Sun-Maid publishes a series of wartime recipe books emphasizing that cooks can save on sugar by using raisins, which already contain natural sugars. Sun-Maid raisins are used to sustain troops and are prized in the field for providing high energy value, great portability, and a long shelf life.

1930 1933—President Roosevelt initiates New Deal   1939—World War II begins   1945—End of World War II

1942
Facing a workforce reduction during World War II, Sun-Maid enters into a cooperative sales and distribution agreement with H.J. Heinz Co., which is later terminated after the war.

1937
One of the New Deal milestones, the Federal Agriculture Marketing Agreement Act is approved. The California Marketing Act is approved by the State Legislature, paving the way for growers to organize for their mutual benefit and to improve the marketing conditions for California raisins.

1951
The California Raisin Advisory Board (CALRAB) is formed for researching, advertising, and promoting California raisins. While the RAC concentrates on quality standards and product volume, CALRAB's focus is on boosting consumption and sales of California raisins.

Raisin Advisory Board Will Form On November 8th

The new California Raisin Advisory Board, made up of both growers and packers, will be organized at a meeting November 8th at 10 AM in the Californian Hotel.

The meeting date was announced today by Paul L. Johnson, the board manager. Grower members and alternate members of the board are being nominated in a series of growers meetings, which will close Thursday night.

Packers Will Nominate

The packers will nominate their seven board members and seven alternates at a meeting

1956
The Sun-Maid Girl keeps up with the times as the trademark undergoes its second modification.

1964
Situated on 73 acres, the 640,000-square-foot Sun-Maid plant opens and is voted one of America's top new plants by *Factory Magazine*.

1956—Federal-Aid Highway Act   1962—Cuban Missile Crisis   *1965*

Raisin Men Okeh Market Plan By 83 Per Cent Vote

Secretary of Agriculture Charles F. Brannan today announced grower approval of the first federal marketing agreement for raisins in the history of the industry.

The secretary told Congressman Cecil F. White of the ninth, Fresno, district 83 per cent of the growers who voted in a referendum last month approved the federal program.

The affirmative votes were cast

1949
Federal and state marketing orders for raisins are approved. The Raisin Administrative Committee (RAC), a cooperative comprising all California raisin producers and handlers, is established with the objective of setting industry-wide quality standards and volume controls.

1961
Sun-Maid Chairman A.E. Swanson breaks ground for a new plant facility in Kingsburg, California.

1956
The RAC establishes minimum grade and condition standards for the California raisin industry.

Sun-Maid Timeline 1965–1995

1977
Premium dried apricots are added to the Sun-Maid product line.

1970
The Sun-Maid logo is once again modernized into the form it would keep into the 21st century.

1976
Sun-Maid begins producing high-proof alcohol from raisin by-products at a distillery facility.

1978
Sun-Maid adds prunes to its product line.

1965 **1969—U.S. puts man on moon** **1971—First e-mail transmission** **1973—First cell phone call**

1967
A group of raisin growers not associated with Sun-Maid form the Raisin Bargaining Association (RBA). Sun-Maid becomes a signatory packer in 1988, allowing the purchase of raisins from RBA growers.

1972
A severe spring freeze on March 27 and 28 spells early disaster for the 1972 raisin crop, which suffers a 60 percent loss to make it the smallest raisin crop since the turn of the century.

An Analysis:
THE FROST OF 1972
PETE CHRISTENSEN
FRESNO COUNTY FARM ADVISOR

What a lousy start! It all began with the late 1971 harvest and the early freeze on October 29 and 30. This caught many vines poorly prepared for winter, particularly some young, one and two-year-old vines which were frozen back to ground level. Cane selection was also poor in many vineyards.
We were also badly shorted on rainfall this winter; many herbicide applications had no beneficial rain. The dry winter is also blamed for some of the "delayed growth" or slow bud break in Thompsons this spring.

6. High covercrop with moist soil
7. Firm but dry soil with and without ground cover
8. Freshly worked dry soil
Advice on how to handle the frosted grapevines was quite abundant and varied. Unfortunately, a Thompson Seedless crop cannot be improved by any special practices such as the removal of frosted shoots. Pruning the canes back may be of value on weak or 3-year-old Thompson vines to promote more shoot growth from the head of the vines for next year's
However, Thompson vines

1971
Sun-Maid helps to establish Sunland Marketing, Inc. to gain marketing leverage and provide the grocery trade with a full line of dried fruit products.

1976
Harvest rains devastate the San Joaquin Valley raisin crop in 1976, and again in 1978 when about 70 percent of the crop is lost.

1986
The California Dancing Raisins are introduced by the California Raisin Advisory Board and earn CALRAB substantial licensing royalties.

1980
Sun-Diamond Growers of California is formed, joining Sun-Maid with fellow co-ops Sunsweet Growers Inc. and Diamond Walnut Growers, Inc. The partnership lasts two decades.

LATE 1980s
Sun-Maid growers begin experimenting with dried-on-the-vine (DOV) raisin production and harvesting. Assuming the leadership role in the effort, Sun-Maid receives a patent for a DOV trellising system in 1995.

1992
Marketing students at California State University, Fresno build and fill the world's largest raisin box, earning a spot in *The Guinness Book of Records*. The box measures 12 feet high, 8 feet wide, and 4 feet deep, and is filled with 16,500 pounds of Sun-Maid raisins. The box is later installed at the Sun-Maid headquarters in Kingsburg.

1980—Smallpox eradicated   1990—World Wide Web debuts   1994—Nelson Mandela elected President of South Africa   *1995*

1980
The carton can is launched.

1988
In connection with Sun-Maid's 75th Anniversary, the original Sun-Maid bonnet worn by Lorraine Collett is donated to the Smithsonian Institution in Washington, D.C.

1980
Sun-Maid raisin bread is introduced as a licensed product.

1994
CALRAB, then a program jointly funded by raisin growers and packers, is terminated by the actions of 15 raisin packers not affiliated with Sun-Maid.

Packers to dissolve CALRAB

■ Petition submitted from 15 raisin packers to terminate the board on July 31.

By Benjamin Seto
The Fresno Bee

It may be a while before the California Raisins dance again.

Enough signatures have been collected from raisin packers to terminate the California Raisin Advisory Board, the industry marketing organization that handles the high-profile dancing raisins advertising campaign.

A Clovis lawyer says he has collected enough signatures from raisin packers to terminate the California Raisin Advisory Board, the industry marketing organization that handles the high-profile dancing raisins advertising campaign.

The action puts into question the future of the

board's 14 full- and part-time employees at its Fresno headquarters and of this fall's multimillion-dollar raisin promotion.

CALRAB's troubles are the latest in a continuing shakeup of fruit-marketing programs in California.

Clovis lawyer Brian Leighton this week submitted a petition from 15 raisin packers — or 75 percent of the 20 member packers — to terminate the board by the end of the current crop season on July 31.

Although sanctioned by the state, these marketing boards, or marketing orders, are run by the industry and may be terminated at any time by 51 percent of the packers who together produce more than 51 percent of the tonnage.

The petition affects only the state order. A

Please see Raisins, Page B9

Sun-Maid Timeline 1995–Present

1998

It takes four years before a consensus is reached for a new state marketing order (The California Raisin Marketing Board), which is funded exclusively by raisin growers.

Raisin market order approved

State growers overwhelmingly support the plan for campaigns.

BY DENNIS POLLOCK
THE FRESNO BEE

Thanks to an industry vote, California's Dancing Raisins could make a comeback, but it's unlikely they'll be dancing.

More likely to be dancing this week are the people who spearheaded a referendum to create promotional and education campaigns aimed at shoppers and industrial raisin buyers.

A new state marketing order for the industry was approved by 87% of those who voted.

"We are pleased that the growers see the program as an opportunity to sell more raisins and that they expressed their support," by such a wide majority, said Vaughn Koligian, executive director of the Fresno-based Raisin Bargaining Association.

The California Department of Food and Agriculture announced results of the referendum:

■ Of 3,771 growers eligible to vote, 2,672 — amounting to 71% — cast ballots.

■ There were 2,294 votes in favor, 328 against.

"I was very pleased at these percentages," said Pete Penner, vice chairman of the Raisin Administrative Committee and chairman of the Sun-Maid Growers of Directors.

"What we've lacked in this industry is togetherness for a common goal. We should do better."

Declining raisin sales — especially on the domestic side — were at the center of the effort to put the marketing program in place. To make it happen, Koligian and Sun-Maid Growers president Barry Kriebel set aside some strong differences on the new program's predecessor, the California Raisin Advisory Board. The board was dissolved in 1994.

The two cooperatives represent 70% of the states' raisin growers.

Jerry Rehrmeier, who heads the much smaller Fresno Cooperative Raisin Growers, said he thinks both growers and packers should be helped by the grower-only marketing order.

"If there is an increase in sales, there will be a better return to the grower, and the packer will be able to increase his price," said Rehrmeier who grows raisin grapes in the Biola area.

Rehrmeier said domestic sales will be an emphasis and "we will be looking for a 'rainmaker', a strong domestic marketing manager who can make it happen."

Penner said that if the Dancing Raisins return, he would expect they would sit this one out — as well-known.

Please see Raisins, Page C2

2001

The United States Department of Agriculture (USDA) releases the Selma Pete variety in 2001.

1997

California EPA recognizes Sun-Maid for its innovative Integrated Pest Management program.

1999

Simon and Schuster Children's Publishing Division publishes *Sun-Maid Raisins Play Book*.

1995   **1995—Amazon.com and eBay are founded**   **1997—Mars Pathfinder lands on Mars**   **1999—World population reaches 6 billion**

1999

The full line of Sun-Maid specialty fruit is expanded.

2000

The Sun-Maid Collectible Doll is issued by the Alexander Doll Company, New York.

2003

Using the trademark colors of red and yellow, Sun-Maid's packaging is redesigned to create a unified look across the brand, which has been further expanded to include more dried fruits.

1995

Sun-Maid milk chocolate covered raisins are introduced as a licensed product.

2005

Sun-Maid meets the needs of the organic-focused consumer by offering a variety of retail packs of Organic Raisins. Sun-Maid is at the forefront of sustainability initiatives and continues to utilize best practices in the manufacturing industry to reduce its carbon footprint.

2006

For the first time, the Sun-Maid girl is animated for print and television ads, and on the newly redesigned website, which features the message highlighting that natural raisins are "Just Grapes & Sunshine®."

2010

Sun-Maid continues to develop its online presence at www.sunmaid.com, including versions in Spanish, bilingual English/ French Canadian, and Japanese. In 2010, Sun-Maid launches a site on Facebook, reaching more customers through social media.

2007—The European Union expands to 27 member states   **2010—33 miners freed from Chilean mine**   *2011*

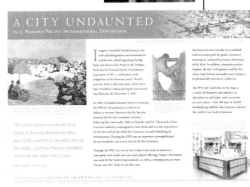

2005

A joint publication of Sun-Maid and Gooseberry Patch features family-friendly recipes with Sun-Maid raisins and dried fruits. Recipes include raisin bread french toast, turkey and wild rice salad, and yogurt-curry chicken salad sandwiches.

2007

Reader's Digest magazine names the Sun Maid Girl® on the red box the "Best lasting logo" as part of its "America's Best" awards. References to the Sun-Maid brand or a close representation continue to be featured in pop culture including *The Simpsons*, *Sesame Street*, and a MasterCard "Priceless" commercial.

2011

Sun-Maid contributes to the restoration efforts of San Francisco's Palace of Fine Arts, the only remaining building from the Panama Pacific International Exposition held in 1915. Sun-Maid's participation in the exposition nearly 100 years prior is highlighted on a series of interpretive panels surrounding the renovated buildings.

The Uses of Raisins

About half of Sun-Maid raisins are packaged and sold in our familiar consumer packages—the other half are sold for use as an ingredient in a wide assortment of food products.

Sun-Maid raisins are the most economical dried fruits around. Available year-round, raisins are easy to use in a wide variety of foods. Cereals, breads, cookies, candies, energy snacks—the raisin is one of the world's most versatile food ingredients!

Commercial customers choose Sun-Maid for quality, consistency, and our ability to meet precise specifications for size, special coatings, and moisture levels.

We also coordinate shipments to meet just-in-time delivery schedules. Most of all, Sun-Maid offers real-world expertise in helping our commercial customers effectively meet their needs.

CEREALS, BAKED GOODS, & GRANOLA BARS

Raisins provide more than just flavor to the cereals and baked goods available at grocery stores today. Using raisins helps bakers reduce or eliminate the use of preservatives in their products, as the propionic acid found in raisins acts as a natural preservative. Another naturally occurring acid in raisins, tartaric acid, enhances the flavor of baked goods and can help reduce the amount of salt needed to flavor breads, cakes, cookies, and pastries.

CONFECTIONARY

Yogurt covered raisins, chocolate bars with raisins, and chocolate covered raisins are just some of the confectionary items using raisins. Chocolate coated raisins are *panned* in large rotating copper kettles.

MIXES

Mixtures of raisins, dried fruits, and nuts are another top use of raisins. Dried fruit mixes are considered an ideal exercise snack because they help to provide sustained energy in a compact and easy-to-carry form.

FLAVOR ENHANCEMENT

Raisins add flavor and texture to foods. Two raisin products—raisin juice concentrate and raisin paste—are flavor enhancers found in everything from breads and cakes to cookies and sauces.

Raisin Juice Concentrate

Raisin Paste

SAUCES

Many well-loved barbecue and steak sauce brands on the market today combine raisin paste and raisin juice concentrate with other ingredients like tomato paste, soy sauce, and vinegar to create a wide selection of bold sauces.

The Uses of Raisins

GRANOLA BARS

First came granola, then came the granola bar, which took the mixture of rolled oats, honey, raisins, dried fruit, and nuts, and made it compact and portable.

TOP 15 RECIPES AT WWW.SUNMAID.COM
1. Classic raisin oatmeal cookies
2. Banana French toast
3. Low-fat raisin oatmeal cookies
4. Broccoli pasta toss
5. Tropical pasta salad
6. Snickerdoodles
7. Maple glazed baked apples
8. Cinnamon raisin scones
9. Cinnamon raisin bread
10. Raisin pie
11. Raisin bread pudding
12. Cinnamon raisin quick bread
13. Banana raisin loaf
14. Breakfast bars
15. Coleslaw

CLASSIC COLESLAW

Raisins add sweetness and texture to classic coleslaw, which combines thinly sliced or shredded cabbage with carrots, mayonnaise, sugar, and vinegar, and can include other fresh fruits such as apples.

CELERY STICKS

Raisins top celery sticks spread with peanut butter or cream cheese, resulting in a sweet, savory, crunchy snack.

RAISIN CARROT SALAD

Raisins join with grated carrots and mayonnaise or yogurt to create this classically simple salad. Some recipes add other ingredients including celery, chopped walnuts, diced apples, or crushed pineapple.

THE USES OF RAISINS

RAISIN STUFFING

Raisins help balance the savory flavors of stuffing made with dried bread or bread cubes, herbs, and spices. Regional variations can determine whether it is called stuffing, filling, or dressing, but the side dish usually accompanies roast turkey and other poultry.

RAISIN OATMEAL COOKIES

Soft, chewy, and delicious, raisin oatmeal cookies are one of the most popular cookies in America. The classic recipe for these easy-to-make favorites is Sun-Maid's most-downloaded recipe at www.sunmaid.com.

BREAD PUDDING

Bread pudding is made from bread that is usually soaked in eggs, cream, sugar, and spices before being baked. Many recipes add raisins or dried fruits, while others incorporate raisin bread.

The Raisin Cereal Story

While cereal might seem like the quintessential breakfast food of today, the first cereals weren't introduced until the late 1800s. Following the invention of the first machines that could shred whole wheat, C.W. Post's cereal company was founded in 1895, W.K. Kellogg invented corn flakes in 1898, and Swiss physician Maximilian Bircher-Benner developed Muesli around 1900.

The new cereals, many of which were first marketed to ease health problems, were a departure from heavier, meat-based breakfasts. Consumers began to embrace the lighter, grain-based offerings, to which the addition of raisins was a natural fit, as seen in the 1928 Sun-Maid ad (*right*). In 1926, Skinner's Raisin Bran was the first raisin bran on the market, and though the term "raisin bran" was once trademarked, it now refers to any bran and raisin cereal.

The Uses of Dried Fruits

Dried fruits have been popular throughout the world for centuries as ingredients appropriate for breakfast, lunch, dinner, snacks, festivals, and special occasions. They are minimally processed, which preserves the natural wholesomeness of the fresh fruits from which they are made, and are a good value compared with more expensive fresh, frozen, and canned fruits. Available in a variety of forms, such as whole, halves, and diced, dried fruits offer limitless creativity when used in recipes and cooking. Today, more than 90 percent of dried fruits consumed in the United States come from California.

FRUITCAKE
Fruitcake is made with chopped dried fruits, nuts, spices, and is sometimes soaked in spirits. Often served during Christmas celebrations and in some parts of the world, weddings, fruitcake has many variations depending on the culture. It can be dense and rich, which is how it is often made in the United States and the Caribbean, or light and airy, as it is in parts of Central Europe.

HOLIDAY FRUIT TRAYS
Carefully arranged dried fruits and nuts make beautiful, delicious, and nutritious gifts. Thanks to the wide availability of dried fruits, consumers around the world enjoy California fruits, many of which are in season for only a short period, any time of the year.

DICED APPLES
The uniform shape of diced dried apples makes them easily combined in recipes for muffins, trail mixes, and granola.

DICED APRICOTS
Home cooks dice apricots into pieces ideal for baking and salads by either first oiling the blade of a knife or with kitchen shears wiped with a small amount of cooking oil.

ROAST GOOSE WITH PRUNES ON SAINT MARTIN'S DAY

Saint Martin's Eve and Day are celebrated on November 10 and 11 in several European countries by eating a roast goose stuffed with prunes and apples. A Danish legend tells that Saint Martin was hiding in a barn when a goose gave away his presence, which is why the bird lost its neck and is eaten on Mortensaften. In Germany, another legend says that the saint died after eating an entire goose in a single meal, which is why the meal is eaten during Martinfest.

FIG PASTE

Different fig varieties, including Mission and Calimyrna figs, are used to make fig pastes ranging in color and consistency.

PRUNE PASTE

Ground prunes have a variety of uses in baking and prepared foods, and they are even a key ingredient in baby foods.

PRUNE JUICE

Made from dried plums that have been softened through steaming and pureeing, prune juice is a source of potassium and helps to maintain digestive health.

CHOPPED DATES

Chopped dates are used to top hot and cold cereals and in cookies, cakes, muffins, and breads.

CHOCOLATE-DIPPED DRIED FRUITS

Apricots, prunes, and dates are covered with chocolate and yogurt in a variety of confectionery items.

Festivals & Holidays

No matter the country or culture, festivals and holidays are most often accompanied by special foods and feasts. Raisins and dried fruits often play an important part of holiday traditions. Though the dishes vary greatly across the globe—from flaky pastries to rich puddings and spiced breads—there are raisin and dried fruit recipes for every celebration and religion.

CHINESE NEW YEAR

One of the most important holidays of the year in China, the Chinese Lunar New Year, is celebrated between late January and mid-February. *Babaofan*, or eight treasure rice pudding, is served during the new year celebration and made with sticky rice and eight different dried fruits and nuts such as raisins, lotus seeds, dates, wolfberries, red beans, and sunflower seeds.

EASTER AND HOT CROSS BUNS

A British specialty traditionally eaten on Good Friday, hot cross buns are made with a spiced dough that includes raisins and is marked with a cross at the top, which can be made from pastry, icing, or two intersecting cuts. There are many superstitions surrounding hot cross buns. One notion is that by sharing one with a friend, their friendship is ensured throughout the year. Others say that taking the buns on sea voyages prevents shipwrecks, and that hanging the buns in a kitchen both prevents fires and aids in the creation of perfect breads.

CARROT CAKE AT EASTER

Many American Easter celebrations incorporate the Easter Bunny, who is said to hide candy-filled eggs and other gifts for children to find during Easter egg hunts. Carrot cake, which can be eaten any time of the year, often includes raisins and is a tradition during Easter—with a nod to rabbits and one of their favorite foods: carrots.

CAPIROTADA FOR LENT

Capirotada is a Mexican bread pudding traditionally eaten during Lent. The pudding is made of bread, sugar, cheese, and raisins. One of the key differences that makes this dish stand out from European bread puddings is the step of soaking the bread in a syrup made from *piloncillo*, which is a solid piece of sugar made by boiling sugarcane, along with cinnamon and nutmeg.

PURIM AND PASSOVER

Part of the Jewish menu during Purim, *hamantashen* (*above*) are three-cornered cookies that can be filled with prunes or dates. Raisins are a part of other Jewish holiday food traditions including *rugelach* for Chanukah and raisin noodle *kugel* for Passover. The Passover Seder (*left*) is a ritual feast eaten to begin the holiday.

Celebrating Dried Fruits in the United States

Apricot Day January 9
Cherry Month February
Hot Cross Bun Day Good Friday (March or April)
Fruit Compote Day March 1
Oatmeal Cookie Day March 18
Chocolate Covered Raisin Day March 24
Raisin and Spice Bar Day April 5
Raisin Day April 30
Raisin Week 1st week in May
Gingerbread Day June 5
Rice Pudding Day August 9
Eat a Peach Day August 22
Cinnamon-Raisin Bread Day September 16
Apple Month October
Four Prunes Day October 17
Mincemeat Pie Day October 26
Raisin Bread Month November
Fig Week 1st week in November
Raisin Bran Cereal Day November 15
Eat a Cranberry Day November 23
Fruitcake Month December
Date Nut Bread Day December 22
Fruitcake Day December 27

Festivals & Holidays

CHILDREN'S DAY IN JAPAN

While the New Year celebration (January 1) is Japan's biggest holiday of the year, another widely celebrated Japanese holiday is Children's Day, or *Kodomo no hi*, observed on May 5. The day is part of the Golden Week, a collection of several national holidays within seven days. For Children's Day, families raise carp-shaped flags called *koinobori* for each member of the family.

HALLOWEEN

Observed on October 31, the holiday is celebrated in the United States and Canada by children wearing costumes and going trick-or-treating, or door-to-door collecting candy. While these traditions have gained popularity elsewhere around the world, some other cultures celebrate All Saints' or All Souls' Day on November 1 and 2, respectively.

RAMADAN

Ramadan is the ninth month of the Islamic calendar and lasts between 29 and 30 days. The observance of Ramadan varies, moving backwards about 11 days each year, depending on the moon. Fasting occurs during the daylight hours. Traditionally, dates are offered to break the fast each night. The festival of fast-breaking, Eid-al-Fitr, occurs at the end of the holy month, and includes special Eid cookies called *ka`ak* containing dates.

CANADIAN THANKSGIVING

In Canada, Thanksgiving occurs on the second Monday in October, and it is a holiday to give thanks and mark the close of the harvest season. Butter tarts are a traditional Canadian Thanksgiving dessert, and are made of butter, sugar, and eggs inside a pastry shell. The filling is similar to the base of a pecan pie, but instead of pecans, butter tarts use raisins and can also include butterscotch, peanut butter, nuts, and maple syrup.

DIWALI, THE FESTIVAL OF LIGHTS

Diwali is popularly known as the "festival of lights" and is a five-day festival in Hinduism, Jainism, and Sikhism, celebrated between mid-October to mid-November. A dessert enjoyed during feasts and celebrations including Diwali is *kheer,* a sweet pudding made from rice and milk and flavored with cardamom, raisins, and nuts.

THANKSGIVING IN THE UNITED STATES

In the U.S., Thanksgiving Day is celebrated on the fourth Thursday of November. The holiday is typically marked by family gatherings and big dinners, often featuring roast turkey, mashed potatoes, and other seasonal favorites including yams and pumpkin pie. Many dinners also include stuffing made with raisins.

CHRISTMAS PUDDING IN THE UNITED KINGDOM

Traditionally served on Christmas Day in the United Kingdom, Christmas pudding is a steamed dessert full of dried fruits, including raisins. Christmas pudding is known for its dark appearance, which comes from the sugars used and the dish's long cooking time. As a special tradition, some people bake small mementos inside the pudding to bring good luck to their guests.

Fresh Fruit Made Into Dried Fruit

Traditional dried fruits are fruits where much of their water content has been evaporated during drying. No sugar or fruit juice concentrates are added. Dried fruits are good sources of essential nutrients, especially potassium and dietary fiber, and they contain a range of increasingly important bioactive phenolic compounds as well as vitamins and minerals unique to each fruit.

One of the common problems encountered with comparing fresh foods to dried foods is the practice of equating on a weight for weight basis, for example, per 100 grams. Not surprisingly, the sugar content of dried fruits versus fresh fruits on this basis appears disproportionately high, contributing to a misunderstanding of the sugar concentration of dried fruits. When portion size and water content are taken into account, natural fruit sugars and calories are equal for fresh and dried fruits.

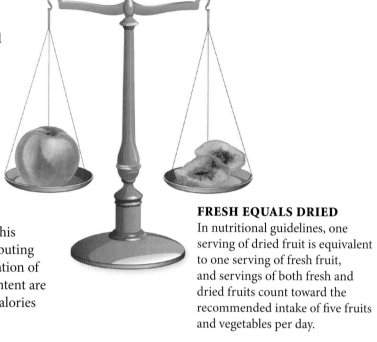

FRESH EQUALS DRIED
In nutritional guidelines, one serving of dried fruit is equivalent to one serving of fresh fruit, and servings of both fresh and dried fruits count toward the recommended intake of five fruits and vegetables per day.

APRICOTS

180g Fresh
(Approximately
3 small apricots) **=**

CALORIES 100 **SUGAR** 21g **FIBER** 12% daily value (DV)
POTASSIUM 11% DV **CALCIUM** 4% DV **IRON** 6% DV

= **40g Dried**
(Approximately
3 dried apricots)

PLUMS & PRUNES

190g Fresh
(Approximately
3 small plums) **=**

CALORIES 100 **SUGAR** 15g **FIBER** 11% daily value (DV)
POTASSIUM 8% DV **CALCIUM** 2% DV **IRON** 2% DV

= **40g Dried**
(Approximately
3 prunes)

GRAPES & RAISINS

170g Fresh
(Approximately
a handful) **=**

CALORIES 130 **SUGAR** 29g **FIBER** 9% daily value (DV)
POTASSIUM 9% DV **CALCIUM** 2% DV **IRON** 6% DV

= **40g Dried**
(Snack size
raisin box)

APPLES

200g Fresh
(Approximately
1 large apple) **=**

CALORIES 120 **SUGAR** 22g **FIBER** 8% daily value (DV)
POTASSIUM 7% DV **CALCIUM** 1% DV **IRON** 2% DV

= **40g Dried**
(Approximately
8 dried apple slices)

FIGS

150g Fresh
(Approximately
5 small figs) **=**

CALORIES 110 **SUGAR** 20g **FIBER** 20% daily value (DV)
POTASSIUM 7% DV **CALCIUM** 6% DV **IRON** 6% DV

= **40g Dried**
(Approximately
5 dried figs)

PEACHES

160g Fresh
(Approximately
1 medium peach) **=**

CALORIES 100 **SUGAR** 17g **FIBER** 14% daily value (DV)
POTASSIUM 12% DV **CALCIUM** 2% DV **IRON** 8% DV

= **40g Dried**
(Approximately
2 dried peach halves)

Making Sense of Serving Sizes

As simple as it seems, many people fail to realize that small children should eat smaller portions compared to adults. The graph on the opposite page illustrates the concept that as children grow to become young adults, they should progressively eat more, and that once they reach full development, decrease the amount they eat.

Child Burger

Youth Burger

Adult Burger

MATCHING PERSON SIZE TO SERVING SIZE

In the 1960s, one national fast food chain introduced hamburgers named for different members of the family, which corresponded to the size of the hamburger. While daily calorie needs are dependant on several factors including gender, age, and physical activity level, in general, serving sizes should increase from children to adults, as shown by each hamburger sized for a child, youth, and adult.

SMALL RAISIN BOXES = SIMPLE PORTION CONTROL

At 45 calories each, Sun-Maid's ½-ounce/14 gram Mini-Snacks® are designed to provide the ideal child's serving size of raisins. The boxes can also be used to demonstrate how calorie needs increase for older children, teenagers, and adults, and therefore so does the recommended serving size of raisins. The small raisin boxes make proper portion control as simple as grabbing one, two, or three boxes.

Child's Serving Size (⅓ of Adult's Serving)	**Older Child's Serving Size** (⅔ of Adult's Serving)	**Teenager's Serving Size** (Adult's Serving)	**Teenager's Serving Size** (Adult's Serving)
½ **ounce / 14 grams**	**1 ounce / 28 grams** (½ ounce / 14 gram boxes x 2)	**1½ ounce / 42.5 grams** (½ ounce / 14 gram boxes x 3)	**1½ ounce / 42.5 grams**

Estimated Calorie Needs Per Day*

GENDER	AGE	SEDENTARY	MODERATELY ACTIVE	ACTIVE
FEMALE	2–3	1,000-1,200	1,000-1,400	1,000-1,400
	4–8	1,200-1,400	1,400-1,600	1,400-1,800
	9–13	1,400-1,600	1,600-2,000	1,800-2,200
	14–18	1,800	2,000	2,400
	19–30	1,800-2,000	2,000-2,200	2,400
	31–50	1,800	2,000	2,200
	51+	1,600	1,800	2,000-2,200
MALE	2–3	1,000-1,200	1,000-1,400	1,000-1,400
	4–8	1,200-1,400	1,400-1,600	1,600-2,000
	9–13	1,600-2,000	1,800-2,200	2,000-2,600
	14–18	2,000-2,400	2,400-2,800	2,800-3,200
	19–30	2,400-2,600	2,600-2,800	3,000
	31–50	2,200-2,400	2,400-2,600	2,800-3,000
	51+	2,000-2,200	2,200-2,400	2,400-2,800

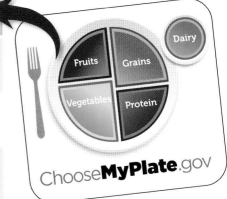

ChooseMyPlate.gov

PROPER PORTION SIZES

The MyPlate food chart issued by the United States government in 2011 focuses on choosing foods from each food group while other guidelines make recommendations for calorie intake. The plate and corresponding portions can be scaled up or down depending on gender, age, and physical activity level.

CALORIES, ENERGY, & SIR ISAAC NEWTON

Sir Isaac Newton's laws of motion laid the groundwork for scientific thinking relating to matter and energy. Calories are units used to measure heat energy, and 1,000 calories equal one kilocalorie, also called a kilogram calorie. Though they are often referred to as calories, it is actually kilocalories that are used to measure food energy.

*Source: *Dietary Guidelines for Americans, 2010.*

CHAPTER 2
The Background Story

History of Raisins & Dried Fruits
Ancient Times

Known to have flourished for 60 million years, wild grapes were discovered by early hunter-gatherers who ate fresh grapes or those dried into raisins by the sun. The earliest cultivated vine was in Anatolia, at the northern peninsula of Western Asia, where wine jars were found dating to 6,000 B.C. Here, in what is now Turkey and the Caucasus, lies Mount Ararat, where, according to the Bible, Noah landed his ark and sowed the first grape seed.

FIT FOR A KING
Remains of engineered irrigation dating to 5,000 B.C. was found along the Nile River, confirming that the Egyptians were cultivating grapes by 3,000 B.C. This painting (*below*) from the tomb of Nakht, in Thebes, shows the gathering and crushing of grapes. Baskets of dried fruits discovered in tombs indicate that Egyptians considered fruit precious goods, worthy of bringing with them into the afterlife.

FORBIDDEN FRUIT
In the Book of Genesis, Adam and Eve ate forbidden fruit from the Tree of Knowledge of Good and Evil. The Latin translation calls the fruit *malum*, which means both "apple" and "evil." Earlier Slavic texts and the *Zohar* (Jewish Kabbalah) describe the forbidden fruit as the grape. Some scholars believe the fruit in question to be the fig, as the next verse describes sewing the fig leaves into loincloths.

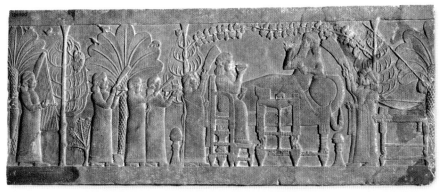

ASSYRIAN STONE RELIEF

Fruit was an important theme for artists in the ancient world, and agriculture was an indication of prosperity. This 7th-century stone relief shows the Assyrian King Ashurbanipal and his queen under grapevines and date palms. By 360 B.C., grapes were common illustrations on Babylonian coins.

AMPHORA

As early as 3,500 B.C., wine and juice were stored and transported in amphora. The grape was prized for its sweetness and made into syrups like *sapa* and *defrutum*, which were common ingredients throughout the classic world. The Greeks frequently decorated their urns with scenes of the grape harvest. Wine stored in an amphora was preserved with a layer of olive oil to keep out the air.

FIGS

The Sumerians were growing figs, dates, plums, and other fruits between the Tigris and Euphrates rivers around 5,500 B.C. Figs were strung together and hung out to dry in long strands, or pressed into cakes that were easily stored and packed for long journeys.

DATES

Arabic legend tells that when man was first created, what remained was used to create the date palm. Today, dates are so widespread that their exact origin is contested by many Middle Eastern, African, and South West Asian countries. It is known that date palms grew in the Jordan Valley as early as 6,000 B.C., and Jericho became known as the "City of Palm Trees." By 3,000 B.C., the date was being cultivated throughout the Fertile Crescent, where its fruit was eaten both fresh and dried. People also ate the shoots and flowers, tapped the sap for syrup, and made household objects using the fiber and wood.

History of Raisins & Dried Fruits
The Old & New World

Dried fruits traveled to new areas across the globe, where they began to be incorporated into diverse cuisines. Knowledge of fruit cultivation and drying expanded and was recorded in greater detail. Greek philosopher Aristotle's writings in his *History of Science* from around 300 B.C. composed a comprehensive system of Western philosophy encompassing morality, aesthetics, logic, politics, metaphysics, and science, including the biology of fruits and seeds and the need to prune vines in order to produce the best fruit. Latin poet Virgil also wrote about making raisin wine in *Georgics*, his four-volume poem from around 29 B.C. Dried fruits traveled to the new world via explorers, and production began in California and Mexico at Spanish missions.

EXPLORATION AND DISCOVERY

According to Nordic legend, Viking explorer Leif Eriksson discovered North America at the end of the 1st century A.D. He landed on a spot teeming with wild grapes and named it Vineland. Archeologists have unearthed what they believe to be that first Norse settlement on the Northern tip of Newfoundland.

FEUDAL SOCIETIES

This illustration of serfs tending to the vineyards of their Manor Lord *(above)* gives a telling account of life in the 12th century. Europe was still in the midst of Catholic military campaigns to control the Holy Land. Crusaders returned from their conquests bearing exotic ingredients and Middle Eastern cooking methods that included the mixing of meat, fruit, and spices. This style of cooking remained fashionable for centuries.

THE RENAISSANCE

Fruit has long been a favorite subject of artists, from the Greeks' rendering of Dionysus on their wine cups to Roman wall paintings at Pompeii and fantastic faces composed entirely of food by Renaissance painter Giuseppe Arcimboldo. This detailed painting, *Still Life of Flowers and Dried Fruit*, from 1611, was painted by Flemish artist Clara Peeters, one of the few known female artists of the time.

20 June 1636. In the Philip of London, master, Robert Huson for New England, John Winthorpe for the Plantation 13 barrel small band pitch, 4½ cwt Raisins, 10 cwt prunes, 5 cwt. sugar, 2 hhds. of vinegar, 38 iron pots and Kettles cost £6. 13s. 4d., iron work value £40. 250 ells of Vitrii canvas, 200 ells packing canvas, 600 ells coarse linen cost 8 pence an ell, several remnants of stuff cost £26, 5 ordinary yard broad sayes, 40 goads Welsh cottons, 14 gross Sheffield Knives, 14 dozen pair shoes with other things.

8. July 1636. In the William and John of London, master, Rowland Langrum for New England: — John Wenthorpe esq for the Plantation at Massachusetts Bay in New England one single serge, 36 yards of flannel, 250 goads Welch cottons, 100 goads Northern cottons, 240 yards ruggs for beds, 7 pair of blankets, 2 cwt. of wrought iron, 200 ells of vittry canvas, 36 pair of canvas breeches cost 45s., 19 cotton waistcoats cost 40s., 108 pair woollen stockings, 3 dozen children's woollen stockings, 40 goads Manchester cottons, 200 yards of Norwich stuffs cost 20 pence a yard, 4 yard broad perpetuances, 8 pieces of Tregar, 20 dozen of shoes, 2 dozen

RAISINS TO THE NEW WORLD

One of the earliest recorded shipments of raisins to the colonies arrived in June 1636. Port records from Boston Harbor show that the governor of the Massachusetts Bay Colony, John Winthorpe, received among his cargo "4½ cwt Raisins." Cwt is the abbreviation for a hundredweight, which is equivalent to about 115 pounds.

ROYAL RAISINS

In the mid–19th century, Queen Victoria's court enjoyed raisins imported from South Africa. When Queen Victoria opened the gardens of Hampton Court to the general public in 1838, the main attraction was a grapevine planted 100 years earlier in Queen Mary's Exotic Plant collection. More than 230 years old, the Great Vine still thrives, and is the oldest and largest known vine in the world. After harvest, visitors can buy the fruit in the palace gift shop.

PRESIDENTIAL FRUIT

In 1754, George Washington began his long residence at Mount Vernon, where raisins were a staple at the dinner table. Dried fruits appeared prominently in his wife Martha Washington's *Booke of Cookery*. When Martha prepared a "plumb broth" made of marrow bones, bread, sugar, raisins, and currants, her husband proclaimed it "the greatest success achieved by Mrs. Washington since our marriage." Following Washington's lead, many favorite dishes of subsequent presidents and first ladies included raisins and dried fruits. Thomas Jefferson returned from France with "figs from Marseilles, raisins, and almonds;" First Lady Dolley Madison was well known for her Scripture Cake featuring raisins and figs; and the Carter family enjoyed carrot and raisin salad.

History of Raisins & Dried Fruits
To California

In 1873, Francis T. Eisen planted an experimental vineyard of Muscat grapes on 25 acres along Fancher Creek, just east of Fresno. In his 1891 publication, *California Homes and Industries*, Eisen described the first production year in 1877:

> *"It was a very hot year, and before the Muscat grapes were harvested a quantity of the crop dried on the vines, and we treated them as raisins, stemmed them, put them in boxes, and sent them to San Francisco market. They were sold to fancy grocers, who exposed them in show-windows and reported them imported from Peru; but a Mr. Hickson found they were from the Eisen Vineyard, and went there to see, and informed raisin dealers that the best raisins were made in Fresno County. Others then entered into the business, and this was the foundation for the present reputation of Fresno for raisins."*

Packaged raisins were shipped out of the state by 1878, and by 1903, California was producing 120 million pounds of raisins a year.

RAISINS OF SPAIN

Spanish artist Joaquin Sorolla y Bastida produced a series of paintings in the 1890s illustrating the raisin industry in Spain. Until the 20th century, the Valencia region of Eastern Spain was a major exporter of raisins. The first raisin grape to be commercially grown in California was the Muscat of Alexandria, brought to the state in 1851 by Colonel Agoston Haraszthy, who discovered it on an expedition overseas.

SUN-DRIED

The photograph below shows apricots and peaches being sun-dried on wooden trays near Sanger, California, circa 1912. Raisins, however, were dried in the field, either on trays or on the vine. While natural seedless raisins are still dried the same way today, most other dried fruits are dried in dehydrators in order to preserve their light color.

PLUMS

In 1850, Frenchman Louis Pellier came to California from Agen, a district known in France as the "Capital of the Prune." He bought a parcel of land near Mission San Jose, and successfully grafted the Agen root stock onto wild plums. In the 1880s, the area experienced a glut of apples and pears, and local growers saw an opportunity for success in the dried plum industry. Dried plums were a popular import, but with the help of the railroad, California soon became the nation's leading producer. By 1900, there were 85 plum-packing plants in the Santa Clara Valley.

APRICOTS

The apricot first arrived in California with Spanish missionaries. Settlers to the Santa Clara Valley, on the southwest tip of the San Francisco Bay, found the area perfect for stone fruit. Plums, peaches, cherries, and apricots thrived in the 1920s, and by 1935 the area had nearly 3,000 apricot growers.

PACKING AND SHIPPING

Packing houses quickly became a vital link between the grower and the consumer, and dozens sprouted up across the San Joaquin Valley. Employing hundreds of people, these facilities received the sun-dried raisins from the grower, then they stored, processed, packaged, and shipped the fruit throughout the United States and to countries around the world.

MUSCAT GRAPES

The large, round berries of the Muscat grape were used to make Fresno County's first raisins. Muscat raisins were the industry standard until the switch to the Thompson Seedless variety.

RAILROADS

The transcontinental railroad was completed in 1869, bringing farmers and immigrants from the East, and enabling growers to quickly transport products from the West to new markets. In 1872, Leland Stanford brought the Central Pacific Railroad to the San Joaquin Valley, choosing a location in present-day downtown Fresno as the rail stop Fresno Station. Depots in surrounding communities, such as the Reedley Depot seen here (*left*), soon followed. As the railroads expanded, so too did the area surrounding Fresno Station, attracting farmers eager to grow agricultural products to satisfy the increasing demand from faraway markets.

History of Raisins & Dried Fruits
To Today

Once Central California's great potential for producing raisins and dried fruits was realized, the area quickly transformed from scattered small farming towns into a top-producing agricultural region. As production increased, so did innovation, and growers, packers, and marketers of raisins and dried fruits all helped establish their industry as a vital part of California's agriculture and economy. Today, California dominates U.S. production, producing more than 90 percent of the nation's raisins and dried fruits.

SHIFTING GROWING AREAS

In 1890, raisin grape acreage was scattered throughout California. By 1950, it had moved to mostly within the San Joaquin Valley and today, most raisin grapes are grown within 50 miles of Sun-Maid's Kingsburg headquarters. The prune and fig industries underwent similar concentrations, and are now grown primarily in the Sacramento and San Joaquin Valleys, respectively.

TOP-PRODUCING CALIFORNIA COUNTIES IN 2010:

Raisins	Prunes	Figs
1. Fresno	1. Sutter	1. Madera
2. Madera	2. Butte	2. Merced
3. Kern	3. Tehama	3. Fresno
4. Tulare		

Prune Production

Raisin Production

DRIED-ON-THE-VINE & MECHANICAL HARVESTING

Growers develop and perfect innovative methods for raisin production such as dried-on-the-vine and mechanical harvesting using continuous trays (*left*).

5 A DAY

Just Eat More
(fruit & veg)

PROMOTING HEALTHY CHOICES

Sun-Maid packages of traditional dried fruits—dried apricots, apples, dates, figs, peaches, raisins, and prunes—include the endorsement of programs encouraging increased consumption of fruits and vegetables: Mix it Up! in Canada, 5 A Day in the United Kingdom, and Fruits & Veggies More Matters in the United States.

CHANGING PUBLIC PERCEPTIONS

In May 2011, internationally recognized health researchers including Dr. Dan Gallaher (*above*), presented their views at the XXX World Nut & Dried Fruit Congress, recommending that food policy-makers consider dried fruits equivalent to fresh fruits in dietary recommendations around the world.

NEW FRUIT VARIETIES

New grape varieties are developed and released, including Fiesta in 1973, DOVine in 1995, and Selma Pete in 2001. These earlier-ripening varieties allow growers to harvest earlier in the season and increase crop yield.

The Golden State

In 1848, gold was discovered at Sutter's Mill, and within a year 300,000 settlers from around the world had come to California to make their fortunes. Gold was found in the San Joaquin River too, and by 1851 the town of Millerton, just north of present-day Fresno, became a bustling mining camp. Soon, much of the California gold had been mined away, and many of the new settlers began to seek alternatives. They were eager to seize opportunities in this sparsely populated region. A second rush to California began, this time for farmland, as the settlers realized the value of the state's warm climate, rich soil, and availability of water. As the new farmers reported their successes to family and friends back home, more immigrants flocked to the state, creating a diverse population with expertise in farming a variety of crops.

THE COLONY SYSTEM

The area experienced a land boom, thanks in part to Martin Theodore Kearney, who began his career in Fresno by managing the Central California Colony for W.S. Chapman and Bernhard Marks of San Francisco. Kearney later promoted developments of his own, including the Easterby Colony east of Fresno and the Fruit Vale Estate west of Fresno. The colony farms offered 20-acre parcels of rich, well-irrigated soil perfectly suited to farming. Immigrants streamed to the area, and by the early 1890s, more than a dozen towns were established, including Caruthers, Centerville, Clifton (now Del Rey), Dinuba, Easton, Fowler, Kingsburg, Reedley, Sanger, and Selma. By the turn of the century, the Valley had been transformed, with the colony farms supporting thousands of fertile acres.

THE VALLEY IS BORN

It has taken millions of years of geologic activity to create the Sierra Nevada mountain range, which is an estimated 40 million years old and contains the popular Yosemite National Park. From the Sierras, ancient glacier runoff has deposited soil in layers on the Valley floor. Mountain rivers and streams have left behind sediment, and formed a wide alluvial plain. A loose mixture of sand, silt, gravel, and clay have created sandy loam, a permeable soil that allows for root expansion and rich nutrients, which provides a fertile growing environment.

PRECIOUS WATER

When the San Joaquin Valley was first settled, farmers relied on rain, and the vast underground water table to nourish their crops. Early man-made canals diverted precious water from the Kings and San Joaquin rivers, and eventually dams allowed snow-pack runoff from the Sierra Nevada mountain range to the east to be better utilized in the Valley fields below.

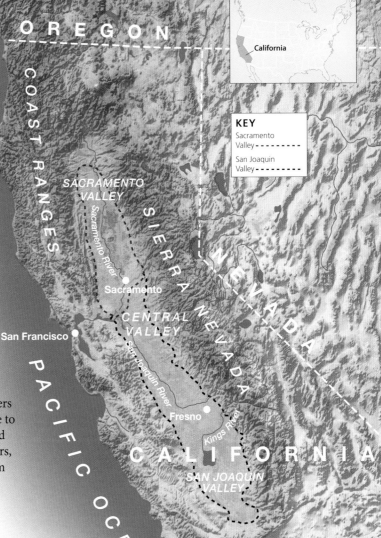

THE IDEAL CLIMATE

California contains several unique micro-climates. The central San Joaquin Valley enjoys optimum weather patterns, contains well-drained sandy loam soil (which dries quickly), and hot, dry Septembers that allow drying grapes to transform into sweet raisins. The mountains surrounding the Valley create a basin of fog during the winter months, allowing fruit crops to rest in dormancy and save their energy for vigorous spring growth. The summer's dry, sunny climate, and fertile soil is tailor-made for dried fruit production. The pioneers of dried-fruit farming realized the potential of this perfect climate. By 1890, California had produced more than 66 million pounds of dried fruits, more than 45 million pounds of raisins, more than 10 million pounds of prunes, and 50,000 pounds of figs.

Irrigation Water

Spanish explorer Gabriel Moraga led an expedition in 1804 to California's interior valley. There, he discovered a large river, and named it San Joaquin for St. Joachim, father of the Virgin Mary. He traveled south through dry grassland and camped along another river on January 6, the day of epiphany. He named it The River of Holy Kings (*El Rio de los Santos Reyes*). Today, the San Joaquin and Kings rivers supply water to one of the most productive agricultural regions in America.

PUTTING WATER TO WORK

The area's first farmers relied on rain and groundwater to nourish their crops. Snow melt from the Sierra Nevada range flows down through the rivers, seeps under the soil, and migrates west to create a vast underground water table in the Valley. The water table was so high that early day farmers could reach it with a shovel. Now, as rain and snowfall fluctuates from year to year, so does the level of the water table. Agriculture began to boom as soon as the flow from the rivers was diverted into dams, irrigation canals, and water districts.

THE FRESNO SCRAPER

Recognizing the need for efficient canal construction, Scottish immigrant James Porteous invented a machine that quadrupled the amount of soil that could be moved by hand. Porteous created Fresno Agricultural Works in the mid-1870s and later patented his "Fresno Scraper." The revolutionary design was used around the world, playing a vital role in the construction of the Panama Canal and digging trenches in World War I. Its design is still referenced for earth-moving machinery today.

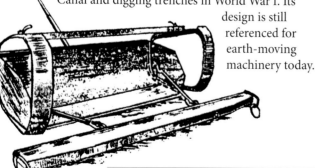

IRRIGATION PIONEERS

In 1868, Anthony Y. Easterby and Moses Church moved from Napa County to Fresno to begin work on an irrigation canal, diverting water into dry fields and producing a beautiful crop. Easterby and Church formed the Fresno Canal and Irrigation Company in 1871—the parent of today's Fresno Irrigation District—which operated roughly 800 miles of canals.

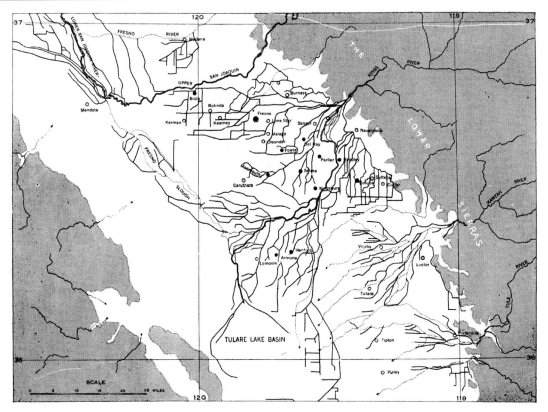

WATER RIGHTS

Once water had been controlled, farmers and ranchers began to argue over their right to it. The Wright Irrigation Act of 1887 permitted farming regions to form irrigation districts. In these districts, small farmers joined together, pooled their resources, and diverted the water to where it was needed. Smaller irrigation districts eventually merged, and today these serve Sun-Maid growers in such districts and associations as the Madera Irrigation District, Fresno Irrigation District, Consolidated Irrigation District, and the Alta Irrigation District.

CENTRAL VALLEY PROJECT

In 1935, the Central Valley Project was created to provide irrigation and municipal water. Water was diverted from various river basins in Northern and Central California by means of canals, aqueducts, pump plants, reservoirs, and dams that, to this day, not only store and manage water but also provide flood control, hydroelectric power, and welcome recreation.

FRIANT DAM

Completed in 1942, the Friant Dam was built across the San Joaquin River, submerging the area's first settlement of Millerton. Water could then flow from Millerton Lake through the Friant-Kern and Madera canals, providing water to Fresno, Kern, Madera, and Tulare counties. Upstream is the Big Creek hydroelectric project, which was created in the 1890s to supply electricity to Southern California.

PINE FLAT RESERVOIR

Construction of the Pine Flat Dam was completed in 1954 by the Army Corps of Engineers. The dam holds back the Kings River as it pours out of Kings Canyon, the deepest canyon in North America. Pine Flat Dam and its reservoir provide flood control, hydroelectric power, and a reliable water source for spring and summer irrigation. This lessens the farmers' reliance on the "run of the river" to deliver their water.

The Thompson Seedless Story

In 1868, English emigrant William Thompson left Illinois with his family, two wagons, and six horses, and crossed the Great Plains into Northern California, settling on a parcel just west of Yuba City. He purchased a number of grapevine cuttings from a nursery back east, three of which are thought to be "Lady de Coverly," described as having originated in Constantinople. He grafted the three cuttings onto his existing root stock. His first vines failed because of a local flood. The remaining vine was overpruned, and produced nothing. Thompson assumed the vine was a dud and ignored it. He later discovered the vine bursting with fruit—and in 1875 it produced 50 pounds of big, sweet, oval grapes with thin skin, low acid, and no seeds.

FINDING THE RIGHT SPOT

The first large vineyard of Thompson's grapes was planted by his friend, J. P. Onstott, on 200 acres in Sutter County. By 1892, Onstott had shipped out thousands of cuttings, many of which ended up in the San Joaquin Valley where grape cultivation was thriving. It didn't take long for growers to identify the Fresno area as a prime grape-growing location.

WHAT'S IN A NAME

William Thompson entered his seedless grape in an agricultural fair at Marysville, a town just east of Yuba City, across the Feather River. He shared the winning root stock with friends, increasing both his popularity and that of the grape. Eventually, his name became synonymous with this grape, which came to be known as the Thompson Seedless. After William Thompson's death, George Thompson, seen in this 1924 photograph tending to grapevines (*right*), worked to keep his father's efforts alive.

CATCHING ON

In 1915, the Thompson Seedless grape was presented at the Panama Pacific International Exposition in San Francisco, where it gained increased consumer attention. While the delicious Muscat raisin was the preferred variety at the time, it contained seeds. When the seeds were mechanically removed, the raisin skin was broken and the fruit became sticky. The Thompson Seedless grape contained no seeds, so the resulting sweet raisin was more convenient to eat. Consumers began to prefer the Thompson Seedless, which quickly became California's most popular raisin grape, now with over 200,000 acres planted statewide. Today, naturally sun-dried raisins made from Thompson Seedless grapes are the preferred raisins for baking, coating with chocolate or yogurt, cereals, and eating out of hand.

Thompson's Seedless Grape

MAKES ABSOLUTELY

⬥ SEEDLESS ⬥ RAISINS ⬥

The very best for Culinary Use !

This Grape has been thoroughly tested in California, having been grown and raisins made of it, in Sutter County, for the past fifteen years.

It is far superior to the Sultana, being much sweeter, a heavier cropper, more easily dried, and ripens earlier.

For rooted vines, guaranteed true to name, address,

B. G. STABLER,

YUBA CITY,

Sutter County, California.

Prices reasonable; given on application for both one and two-year old rooted vines. Will also send *sample of raisins, if desired.*

Picking Thompson Seedless Grapes in California.
Fresno County, Cal.

SPREADING THE WORD

By the 1930s, the Thompson Seedless was well established, and the sunny, agriculturally rich San Joaquin Valley was well known across the country. Postcards of the thriving industry were sent home by visitors, prompting even more migration to the area.

The Fresno MORNING Republican

VOL. LVII—NO. 16. —V—   FRESNO, CALIFORNIA, FRIDAY, JANUARY 16, 1920.   PRICE FIVE CENTS

CONSTITUTIONAL PROHIBITION GOES INTO EFFECT TONIGHT

REPORT MILLIONS INVOLVED; COAST SHIPYARD FRAUDS

WORLD LEAGUE COMES INTO EXISTENCE TODAY

AMERICA PRESENTS 35,000,000 FOREST SEEDS TO EUROPE

REPORT MUTINIES OF FRENCH SERVICE MEN AT TOULON

DUTCH OFFICIALS

GERMAN SOVIETS URGE COUNCILS IN ALL PLANTS

RED SUCCESS RAISES FEAR OF MORE WAR

British Naval and Military Officials Hurry to Paris

SOVIETS CONTROL ALL OF RUSSIA

Attack on Poland Doubted for Strategic Reasons

CANNOT BE MADE, SOLD OR MOVED IN UNITED STATES

No Searching of Houses or Seizure of Stocks Except Where Law Is Violated

Figures Show Remarkable Reduction Already of Petty Crime and Drunkenness

FAREWELLS TO BE GIVEN TO BOOZE TONIGHT

BREWERS STILL HOPE COURTS WILL SAVE THEM

Want "Definition of Intoxicants" Made Illegal

SHOW EXTREME OF ENFORCEMENT

Predict Use of Alcohol as Medicine Will Be Stopped

PROHIBITION

Congress' passage of the Eighteenth Amendment in 1920 prohibited the production and sale of alcoholic beverages. On January 16, 1920, the Fresno Republican reported the new law, and alcohol was dumped into Fresno County's Dry Creek. Prohibition shifted more Muscat grapes, many of which were used for winemaking, into the raisin market. Even with the increased supply of Muscat grapes for raisins, customers clearly preferred the Thompson Seedless. In 1933, Congress passed the Twenty-First Amendment repealing prohibition. The Thompson Seedless had proved to be an ideal grape, due both to consumer preference and growers' desire for a versatile variety usable for both winemaking and raisins.

HISTORIC LANDMARK

Along Colusa Highway (State Highway 20), just west of Yuba City, lies California's official monument to the Thompson Seedless grape. This plaque marks the spot where Thompson propagated the Lady de Coverly grape, later known as the Thompson Seedless.

SUN·MAID®

Puffed Seeded Muscats

REG. U.S.
PAT. OFF

CALIFORNIA
SUN-MAI
SEEDLES

SUN·MAID

SUN-MAI
PUFFEI

CHAPTER 3

The Sun-Maid Story

Sun-Maid Today

Since its beginning in 1912, Sun-Maid has been serving American families and the world. The company experienced interruptions in exports to Europe during World War I, and to the world during World War II. Today, global trade distributes Sun-Maid boxes and packages to over 50 countries.

SUN-MAID HEADQUARTERS

Opened in 1964, the Kingsburg plant was recognized then as one of America's top new plants by *Factory Magazine*. The 640,000-square-foot, state-of-the-art facility sits on more than 100 acres, 20 miles south of Fresno. The facility is continuously improving to meet the demand of customers around the world.

WORLDWIDE SUCCESS

Sun-Maid is one of the world's most recognized brands. Sun-Maid enjoys preferred ingredient supplier status with many domestic and international food-processing companies.

PRODUCT LINE

Sun-Maid offers a full line of dried-fruit products that include raisins and dried fruits, chocolate and yogurt fruits, raisin breads, and baking mixes. Sun-Maid also offers its products in bulk as ingredients for food manufacturers.

FOCUS ON FAMILY

Sun-Maid offers products that appeal to customers of all ages and has partnered with movie and animation studios for family-friendly consumer promotions.

VISITORS WELCOME

Travelers are always welcome at the Sun-Maid plant. Just off Highway 99 in Kingsburg, California, visitors can view the world's largest raisin box and stock up on raisin and dried fruit souvenirs at the Sun-Maid Store.

ADVERTISING

Throughout Sun-Maid's history, unique advertising has made it one of the world's most recognizable and trusted brands. Through television, print media, websites and social networks, promotional products, and recipe books, the Sun-Maid line of products reaches out to consumers worldwide.

Cooperatives

Beginning in Europe as the industrial revolution rapidly transformed society and business, the 1844 establishment of the Rochdale Equitable Pioneers Society in England provided the basis for the growth of the modern cooperative movement.

Sun-Maid cooperative principles allow members to gain through cooperation, sharing in the cooperative's marketing efforts and benefiting from reduced processing and manufacturing costs through economies of scale. Education and technical support assists growers in their own operations, and the democratic process enables self-governance.

Many well-known brands function as cooperatives, including agricultural cooperatives Sunkist Growers, Blue Diamond Growers, Sunsweet Growers, Ocean Spray Cranberries, and Land O'Lakes. Other cooperative organizations include utility cooperatives, supply cooperatives, and credit unions, as well as others including international hotel chain Best Western and the consumers' cooperative Recreational Equipment Incorporated, or REI.

Applied to the raisin industry, advantages of the cooperative include reliability, product control from field to end user, growers having a financial interest in keeping customers satisfied, and the ability to put a face to family farming.

A MEETING OF MINDS

In 1912, a group of California raisin growers created the California Associated Raisin Company, which became Sun-Maid Growers of California. The new organization was intended to combat low prices and fluctuating demand, and to provide better economies of scale in processing, selling, and creating stable markets.

THE RAISIN KING

Several early attempts to organize growers failed, in part because of the rapid growth of the raisin industry. Developer Martin Theodore Kearney proposed pooling resources to improve marketing and distribution. His ideas and leadership gained his election as president of the California Raisin Growers' Association, which was formed in 1895 and incorporated in 1899. After initial success, difficult years followed with the Association's demise in late 1905.

Barton Opera House, Fresno, Cal.

ARMORY HALL

In November 1912, Fresno's Armory Hall served as the site for the organizational meetings of the California Associated Raisin Company, which later became Sun-Maid Growers of California. Armory Hall (foreground) and the Barton Opera House (located at far right) were built in 1889 by vineyardist Robert Barton.

SUN-MAID CITY

By 1918, the booming raisin business needed a new home. Sun-Maid opened a state-of-the-art factory near downtown Fresno. Upon its opening, Sun-Maid City was dubbed the "finest factory building west of Detroit."

MARKETING TO AMERICA

In 1915, the Cooperative hired a national sales team to market raisins directly to grocers. This effort, in conjunction with the introduction of the new Sun-Maid brand, print advertisements, and recipe booklets, significantly increased America's raisin consumption.

The Sun-Maid Girl

Many people want to know if a real person was the original "Sun-Maid Girl." The answer is "Yes," and her name was Lorraine Collett (Petersen). In May 1915, San Francisco was still recovering from its 1906 earthquake and celebrated its rebirth by welcoming the international community to the Panama Pacific International Exposition. Lorraine Collett attended this event with a number of other girls as representatives of the recently formed California Associated Raisin Company, later Sun-Maid Growers of California.

AT THE EXPOSITION

The Sun-Maid girls handed out raisin samples to visitors of the Panama Pacific International Exposition while wearing white blouses with blue piping and originally BLUE sunbonnets.

LORRAINE COLLETT

As Lorraine would later tell, "It was only after we returned to Fresno that I was seen by Sun-Maid executive Leroy Payne wearing my mother's red bonnet in my backyard that the bonnet color was changed from blue to red, because red reflected the color of the sun better."

THE FIRST PAINTING

While working at the Expo in San Francisco, Collett posed at the Post Street studio of artist Fanny Scafford in the morning, then spent the rest of the day working the Expo, where the Sun-Maid girls were by then all wearing RED bonnets. The artist experimented with a variety of positions and props, finally settling on the iconic pose with an overflowing tray of grapes and a glowing sunburst in the background.

TOP STORY

This photograph of Lorraine (far right) appeared in the San Francisco *Bulletin* in 1915 and promoted Sun-Maid's activities at the Exposition.

A NATIONAL TREASURE

In celebration of Sun-Maid's 75th anniversary, the treasured original sunbonnet, by then faded pink, was donated to the Smithsonian Institution in Washington, D.C. on January 26, 1988, in the presence of U.S. Secretary of Agriculture Dick Lyng.

THE RED BONNET

In 1915, life was much simpler, more rural, and sunbonnets were still part of women's fashion in California. Lorraine kept her original red bonnet carefully folded in a dresser drawer from 1915 until she graciously presented it to Sun-Maid in a small ceremony in 1974.

THE ORIGINAL SUN-MAID

After the Exposition, Miss Collett did further modeling and appeared in the 1916 Cecil B. DeMille film *Trail of the Lonesome Pine*. Lorraine Collett Petersen, as she was known after marrying, later became a nurse and until her death at the age of 90, continued to make special appearances as the original Sun-Maid Girl.

The Panama Pacific International Exposition

In 1915, San Francisco hosted the Panama Pacific International Exposition, which celebrated the completion of the Panama Canal and the host city's recovery efforts following a devastating earthquake and fire in 1906. From February to December of 1915, visitors were treated to grand buildings and displays among statues, murals, fountains, lakes, and gardens, including a working model of the Panama Canal and a replica of the Greek Parthenon. Attractions showcased the greatest arts, transportation, machinery, and agriculture of the time—and Sun-Maid had its own exhibit. The exposition lasted nine months and Sun-Maid's wide exposure there helped launch the brand to worldwide recognition.

THE CALIFORNIA BUILDING

Sun-Maid, then known as the California Associated Raisin Company, had its display in the California building within the Exposition's horticultural palace. Other Exposition attractions included exhibits, performances, and parades from countries around the world, as well as American states, counties, and businesses.

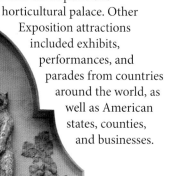

A CITY SHOWCASED

It took three years to construct the 630-acre fairgrounds, which were built on more than 70 cleared city blocks and filled-in mud flats at the northern part of San Francisco, now known as the Marina. The buildings, which were made only to last for the year of the Exposition, were constructed of wood and covered with plaster and burlap fiber that could be molded and sculpted.

RAISIN SEEDER

Sun-Maid's raisin seeder in the horticultural palace was such a popular attraction that a second raisin seeder was added in the food products palace. As part of the live demonstration, Muscat raisins with seeds were placed into the machine, and instantly, seeded raisins came out to be enjoyed by Exposition visitors.

THE FIRST SUN-MAID GIRLS

At the start of the Exposition, Lorraine Collett had yet to pose for the now-famous watercolor that would become Sun-Maid's logo. Throughout the Exposition, Collett (*pictured second from right*) served with other young women as raisin ambassadors, passing out samples of raisins to visitors.

IN THE NEWS

The *Fresno Morning Republican* reported on Exposition events and encouraged local residents to attend special celebrations including Fresno County Day in March, 1915. In turn, the Exposition's Fresno County visitors participated in parades and giveaways of raisins and raisin bread to encourage Exposition visitors to attend Raisin Day festivities held in April, 1915 in Fresno.

SUN-MAID SAMPLES

The Exposition attracted visitors from around the world, many who were only just sampling raisins for the first time. In addition to enjoying raisins, visitors could view what was called a "stereomotograph," a device displaying 3' x 3' three-dimensional scenes of raisin growing and production in the San Joaquin Valley.

THE PALACE OF FINE ARTS

The Palace of Fine Arts is the only remaining building from the 1915 Exposition. With assistance from Sun-Maid, the 2010 Campaign for the Palace of Fine Arts worked to retrofit the building and preserve it for future generations. Today, Sun-Maid's participation in the 1915 Exposition is featured in one of six new interpretative panels surrounding the Palace.

A CITY UNDAUNTED
1915 PANAMA-PACIFIC INTERNATIONAL EXPOSITION

Imagine a beautiful Mediterranean city, with splendid gardens and monumental architecture, stretching along the Bay from Van Ness to Fort Point in the Presidio. Such was the Panama-Pacific International Exposition of 1915, a celebration of the completion of the Panama Canal. The 635-acre fair, built in only four years, drew more than 19 million visitors during its nine month run, February 20–December 4, 1915.

In 1904, city leaders showed interest in hosting the PPIE for the potential of millions of dollars in revenue. However, the fair became essential for the city's economic recovery following the catastrophic 1906 earthquake and fire. The people of San Francisco tirelessly campaigned to raise funds and win the commission for the fair; and all the while San Francisco was still rebuilding its infrastructure. Hosting the PPIE was an impressive accomplishment by any standards, and a near miracle for San Francisco.

Through the PPIE, the city by the Golden Gate made its mark as a metropolis with world-class arts and cultural offerings. Many Californians saw work by the French Impressionists, as well as contemporary art from Europe and New York, for the first time.

San Francisco also was able to re-establish itself as a major port for global commerce, ensuring its continued economic dominance of the West. In addition, abundant produce displays, the fair's lush gardens and the Bay Area's mild climate persuaded many fairgoers to permanently relocate to California.

The PPIE put California on the map as a center for business and industry, an ideal place to call home, and a nexus for art and culture. After 288 days of 70,000 breathtaking exhibits, San Francisco showed the world it was back in business.

"*The Canal means more to the West Coast of America than to any other part of this country or any other part of the world…and San Francisco probably represents the whole West Coast.*"

PRESIDENT TAFT, 1911

THIS PANEL A GIFT OF SUN-MAID GROWERS OF CALIFORNIA

Building the Brand

Since 1912, advertising had been the key to Sun-Maid's success. Almost immediately, ads featured in newspapers and magazines quickly turned Sun-Maid into a nationally recognized brand.

BEAR BRAND

Before it was Sun-Maid, raisins sold by the California Associated Raisin Company were packaged under the Bear brand trademark, referencing the state's Bear Flag. In 1914, advertising manager E. A. Berg originated the Sun-Maid brand name. Inspired by the natural sun-dried raisin process, he adapted the slogan "made in the sun" to Sun-Maid.

THE RAISIN TRAIN

The first major advertising campaign was created when a train loaded with 1,250 tons of raisins headed to Chicago, festooned with signs reading "Raisins Grown by 6,000 California Growers." For 2,000 miles, the Raisin Train piqued the country's interest in both raisins and California.

ANITA KING

An actress, stunt-car driver, and the first woman to drive alone across America, Anita King was a well-known celebrity in 1915 when she visited Fresno to participate in a Sun-Maid advertising campaign. Dressed in a Sun-Maid red bonnet, Miss King sat for photos, ate raisin pie, and rode through town in a fire engine.

RAISIN DAY

Fresno held its first Raisin Day Parade on April 30, 1909. The event was a huge success and drew 100,000 people. Visitors enjoyed contests, races, performances, and the parade, which boasted float entries from community groups, businesses, townships, and counties as far away as Los Angeles, and became an annual event.

THE SUN-MAID BRAND

By the early 1920s, the California Associated Raisin Company's membership comprised 85 percent of the state's raisin growers. The organization changed its name to Sun-Maid Growers of California in 1922 to identify more closely with its nationally recognized brand.

RAISIN RECIPES

Sun-Maid created interest in raisins with print ads in national publications. The repeated message touted the sweet, simple purity of the raisin and its health benefits. Recipes for raisin bread and raisin pies promoted home baking, and prompted people to ask for these products at their local bakeries, which in turn increased sales from wholesale buyers.

1915
The Association began using the "Sun-Maid" brand name and the painting of Lorraine Collett (and when later married, Lorraine Collett Petersen).

1923
The original image of the Sun-Maid Girl was modified for the first time, giving her a bigger smile, brighter colors, and a stylized sun. This more contemporary look kept her in style with the rapidly changing 1920s.

1956
In the mid-1950s, the trademark was updated for the second time. The sun was moved off-center, intensifying the effect of the sunshine with the bonnet casting a shadow across the Sun-Maid Girl's face.

1970
Brighter colors and a geometric sun modernized the logo's third update, with the brand's name now printed in yellow, giving a warmer, sunnier feel. This Sun-Maid Girl continued into the 21st century.

Sun-Maid Advertising

Sun-Maid continued to expand its advertising strategies into the 1930s and beyond, keeping in step with fashions, popular culture, and technology. But regardless of the medium, Sun-Maid's message of flavor and nutrition remained constant.

THE *LADIES' HOME JOURNAL*

Published since 1883, the *Ladies' Home Journal* chronicled American life from the woman's perspective, covering family, marriage, work, home, and beauty issues. Sun-Maid targeted this audience by promoting healthy, sweet raisins for home cooking.

SATURDAY EVENING POST

The most widely circulated publication of its time, the *Saturday Evening Post* appealed to America with its high-quality art, short stories, essays, serialized novels, jokes, cartoons, and poetry. This ad from 1940 depicts raisins used at home, and their appeal to soldiers overseas, who welcomed the non-perishable taste of home.

DOUBLE-DECKER

With bus transportation being a common mode of transportation, Sun-Maid capitalized by advertising in London, England, circa 1932. More raisins were consumed per capita in England than anywhere else, and the British helped to popularize them around the world.

KID APPEAL

The natural appeal of raisins to children has been used consistently in Sun-Maid advertising. This ad promotes raisins as a healthful snack, a precursor to the 1980s "Nature's Candy" marketing campaign.

MAKE A FRESH START.

THE CARTON CAN

The freshness of Sun-Maid raisins became the focus of new packaging in 1980. The carton can's airtight lid kept raisins plump and moist, and the larger opening made it more consumer friendly. The package was an instant hit.

DANCING RAISINS

The California Raisin Advisory Board introduced the California Dancing Raisins in 1986. Images on lunchboxes, notebooks, clothing, posters, toys, and video games earned the California Raisin Advisory Board considerable licensing royalties.

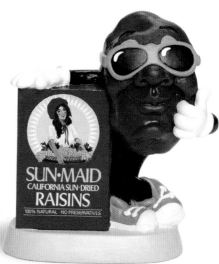

SWEET BY NATURE

A series of television and print ads ran in the 1990s with children as Sun-Maid spokespersons. The ads became one of Sun-Maid's best-loved campaigns.

CELEBRATING YOSEMITE

Sun-Maid celebrated Yosemite National Park's centennial anniversary in 1990 with advertising that showcased Ansel Adams' 1960 photograph *Moon and Half Dome*. Sun-Maid was the first food company to receive permission to use an image from the Ansel Adams Publishing Rights Trust in connection with advertising and promotions.

STAR POWER

In 2006, the Sun-Maid Girl was animated for the first time. Her 21st-century image appeared in print, on television, and on the company's website to launch the new slogan, "Just Grapes & Sunshine®."

Norman Rockwell & Sun-Maid

During the 1920s, renowned artist Norman Rockwell created a series of advertisements which illustrated Sun-Maid's integral place in the traditional American household. These illustrations appeared in the leading magazines of the time, including *Saturday Evening Post*, *Good Housekeeping*, and *Ladies' Home Journal*. As the greatest commercial illustrator of his time, Rockwell's illustration technique was the inspiration behind bringing the Sun-Maid girl to life in 2006.

CELEBRATING SUN-MAID'S 75TH
A collectible plate was produced to commemorate Sun-Maid's 75th anniversary in 1987 featuring the painting *Market Day Special*.

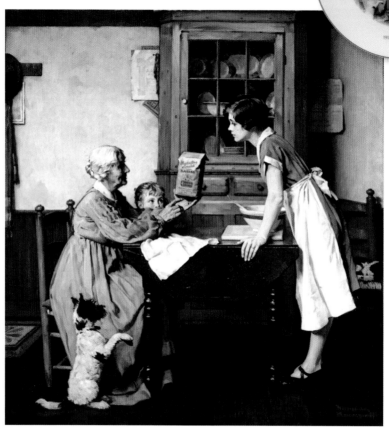

NORMAN ROCKWELL

Rockwell was born in New York city in 1894 and studied art from the age of 14. He became the art director of the Boy Scouts of America publication *Boys' Life* while still in his teens. During his career as a freelance illustrator, Rockwell painted 322 covers for the *Saturday Evening Post* in addition to producing work for *Life*, *Literary Digest*, *Country Gentleman*, and *Look*. Rockwell lived in the New England town of Arlington, Vermont, for years until a fire in 1943 destroyed his studio, along with many paintings. He later moved to Stockbridge, Massachusetts, where he lived until his death at the age of 84. A trust put his art and archives into what would become the Norman Rockwell Museum and his last studio, a red barn-like structure, was moved to the museum grounds in 1986. A celebration to mark the 100th anniversary of Rockwell's birth was held from 1994–1995 at the Norman Rockwell Museum in Stockbridge, Massachusetts. During the celebration, two original oil paintings commissioned by Sun-Maid (*Market Day Special* and *Fruit of the Vine*) were loaned to the museum, where they remain today.

MARKET DAY SPECIAL
The 1927 painting *Market Day Special* measures 35 x 33 inches (89 x 84cm) and features Sun-Maid's economical 4-pound raisin package.

IN A WONDERFUL BARGAIN BAG

Painted in 1927, *In a Wonderful Bargain Bag* measures 30 x 28 inches (76 x 71cm) and features Sun-Maid's blue "Market Day Special" bag.

FRUIT OF THE VINE

Painted in 1926, *Fruit of the Vine* measures 31 x 27 inches (78.5 x 68.5cm) and features Sun-Maid's blue muscat raisin box. In a 1967 letter sent from Norman Rockwell to Sun-Maid, Rockwell explained that the elderly woman in the painting was the mother of his first wife. Rockwell often used family members and people from his community as subjects in his work.

THE MORE RAISINS THE BETTER THE PUDDING

The More Raisins the Better the Pudding was painted in the 1920s and used in a *Saturday Evening Post* advertisement. The painting, measuring 33 x 47 inches (84 x 119cm) was used to feature Sun-Maid raisins in puddings in 40,000 grocery stores.

LITTLE REBELS CAN'T HOLD OUT

Painted in 1928, *Little Rebels Can't Hold Out* was used in a print ad appearing in *The Farmer's Wife*. As in all of his commercial illustrations, Rockwell downplayed the product's prominence and focused on the interaction between generations.

Raisins in Popular Culture

Sun-Maid raisins not only hold a place in history, but also a place in the hearts of children and adults across the globe. Sun-Maid's status as the most well-known and highly regarded name in raisins makes the brand a natural choice to be featured in numerous forms of pop culture.

Throughout the years, Sun-Maid products have appeared on early-morning and late-night talk shows, and even featured in a MasterCard "Priceless" commercial as one of the necessary items for building the best snowman on the block.

Consumers around the world recognize the iconic red raisin box, featuring the bright California sun and the Sun-Maid Girl and red bonnet. Sun-Maid raisins in the red and yellow box are seen everywhere, from children's books and television programs to magazines and video games, all the while evoking the healthful, wholesome qualities embraced by the Sun-Maid brand.

MAD RAISINS

By the fall of 1988, the California Dancing Raisins were at the height of their popularity and appeared on the cover of humor magazine *Mad* alongside the magazine's mascot, Alfred E. Neuman.

SESAME STREET

In 1987, the award-winning children's show *Sesame Street* aired an animated segment evoking the Sun-Maid brand by featuring a woman in a red bonnet. Titled "Snacks on Parade," the cartoon explained Sun-Maid's process of sun-drying raisins, packaging them in red and yellow boxes, and sending them out for the rest of the world to enjoy.

...her take-charge types through a rigorous ten-

(shown above) raised reading scores by 100% in just two years.

An advertising icon since 1916, the Sun-Maid Raisins girl was based on the late Lorraine Collett Petersen, a seeder and picker from Fresno, California, where Sun-Maid began its operations. Though she's undergone some slimming and trimming over the years, she's still the image of outdoorsy good health that raisins, high in antioxidants and natural sugars, represent.

Dra... for a drive... tunne... yours... While... wheels... a bath... stations... shampo... ers ($5 f...

Vote for your favorit...

MONOPOLY

Sun-Maid's library of artwork, advertising, and historical documents provided plenty of colorful material for the Sun-Maid Monopoly game, created in 2006.

AMERICA'S BEST

In 2007, *Reader's Digest* named the Sun-Maid Girl the Best Lasting Logo for its annual "America's Best" issue.

THE SIMPSONS

The 400th episode of *The Simpsons* aired in 2007 and featured Marge baking her famous raisin sponge cake for the Springfield Elementary school bake sale. Finding her carton of "Sun-Made" raisins empty, she went to the grocery store where she fought with Helen Lovejoy over the last box of "Sun-Made" raisins on the shelf.

"I think I need one more thing to make my fruit salad really special," said Blue.

"What about raisins?" said Joe.

Blue thought for a moment. She'd never tasted raisins before.

"Oh, I don't know if I like raisins," Blue said.

"You won't know until you try," said Mrs. Pepper.

Blue agreed and tasted one. "Hey! These are good."

Blue added raisins to their shopping cart, which was full. She had everything she needed for her fruit salad. It was time to head home.

BLUE'S CLUES

The 2007 children's book *Healthy Snacks with Blue!* featured Nickelodeon's favorite dog, Blue, and her friend Joe preparing a healthy snack to share with Blue's class. Blue and Joe use Sun-Maid raisins as one of the ingredients in the fruit salad they make to celebrate "Healthy Snacks Day."

100 Years of Recipe Books

Sun-Maid recipe books offer healthy, imaginative ways to use raisins and dried fruits in everyday meals and for special occasions. Over the course of the past century, Sun-Maid recipes have reflected the changing times, and tastes. During the Great Depression and the following war years, the recipes addressed sugar rationing, and offered a high energy, portable, and well-preserved food for troops fighting overseas. Today, Sun-Maid recipe books include raisin and dried fruit recipes from a variety of ethnic cuisines.

1915

The *Souvenir California Raisin Recipe Book* was distributed at San Francisco's Panama Pacific International Exposition. Its recipes included raisin breads, cakes, cookies, puddings, and pies.

1924

Recipes of this era were primarily baked goods and sweet desserts, with a few sweet relishes, sauces, and spreads, as seen in *Famous Cooks' Recipes for Raisin Cookery*.

1942

Nationwide food rationing created a challenge for cooks during World War II and Sun-Maid's *Wartime Recipes That Taste Good* offered tips for using the natural sugars in raisins.

2006

American tastes have changed over the years, and since the 1960s, ease of preparation for busy, modern families has been key, as seen in the recipe book, *Fruit & Sunshine*.

10 DECADES OF RECIPE ART

Sun-Maid's first cookbooks included color illustrations and over the years, eventually incorporated color photography. While some books offered a wide range of raisin and dried fruit recipes, others focused on specialty topics, including cookies, breads, and holiday favorites.

1915 1916 1920 1921 1922 1923 1924 1925 1926 1927

1928 1930 1931 1932 1942 1943 1944 1949 1955 1960

1964 1980 1987 1989 1990 1992 1993 1995 1996

2001 2002 2002 2005 2006 2007 2007

Nothing beats the power of peanut butter and raisins!

Breezy Breakfast & High Power Snack Ideas:

PBAR Sandwiches (Peanut Butter, Apple and Raisin)
Toast whole wheat bread, spread with peanut butter, sprinkle with Sun-Maid Raisins and top with apple butter.

Nutty Apple Sandwich Prep time: 5 minutes Servings: 1 apple, 8 wedges

1 medium apple
3-4 tablespoons peanut butter
¼ cup Sun-Maid Fruit Bits or Raisins

CORE apple and slice into about 8 wedges.
SPREAD wedges of apple with peanut butter.
TOP each apple wedge with some Fruit Bits or Raisins.
PLACE wedges of apple on plate and serve.

16

Treat yourself to Sun-Maid Raisin Bread slices spread with peanut butter.

Sweets

Spring Flower Cupcakes

Sun-Maid S'mores Bars

PARENTS AND CHILDREN

Since raisins are a family food, Sun-Maid has published recipe books with child-friendly foods and recipes.

Bringing the Sun-Maid Girl to Life

The Girl™ is a dominant part of Sun-Maid's link with consumers. In celebration of her 90th birthday, she was brought to life in March 2006. This was the work of Synthespian Studios, a Massachusetts-based animation company. Launched with a full-page ad in *USA Today* and on the Sun-Maid website, the Sun-Maid Girl was aired on television with the marketing campaign "Just Grapes & Sunshine®" to highlight the natural goodness of raisins. The animated Sun-Maid Girl received national attention,

including articles in the *New York Times*, *Chicago Tribune*, *Philadelphia Inquirer*, *San Francisco Chronicle*, and *Fresno Bee*. While the animated Sun-Maid Girl helped bring raisins into the modern age, she was not designed to replace the Sun-Maid logo—the logo, which has remained the same since 1970, appears on packaging for Sun-Maid products, while the animated Sun-Maid girl appears in television commercials, print advertising, and on the Sun-Maid website.

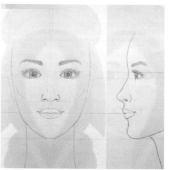

TRUE TO IMAGE
Animation designers worked carefully to stay true to the Sun-Maid Girl's look on packages, which did not change.

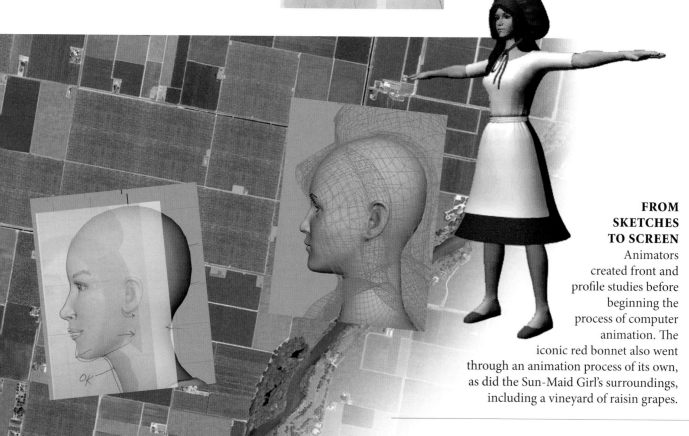

FROM SKETCHES TO SCREEN
Animators created front and profile studies before beginning the process of computer animation. The iconic red bonnet also went through an animation process of its own, as did the Sun-Maid Girl's surroundings, including a vineyard of raisin grapes.

THINKING OUTSIDE THE BOX

Until she was animated, the Sun-Maid Girl lived within the confines of the two-dimensional logo seen on packaging. Not only did the animation process allow her to move through a raisin vineyard, but she could now visit a variety of settings and speak in multiple languages to reach wider audiences. Ads featured her baking in the kitchen, doing yoga on the beach, and at a movie premiere.

THE VINEYARD

Animators studied raisin grapes and vineyards to bring them into the digital world. Photographs of grapes and grapevines were taken so that animators could then produce an entire vineyard.

Sun-Maid Memories

Consumers were asked through Sun-Maid's website and marketing materials to share their favorite Sun-Maid memories. Many consumers responded to the request and their memories are posted on Sun-Maid's website at www.sunmaid.com.

TRYING TO MAKE RAISINS

Mother always had Sun-Maid raisins in the house as long as I can remember. She used them in cookies, breads, cereals, and puddings, and put little boxes of them in our lunch sacks. They have their own smell and look and feel, and they bring back warm feelings of yesteryear. I asked her once what raisins were and she told me they were grapes that had been dried in the sun. I remember going outside and finding a long wooden board and laying it in the sun, and then found a bunch of grapes that I laid one at a time, side by side, on the board. I sat back and waited for them to turn into raisins. They were there the next day too, but they didn't look like the ones in the box.

Thank you, Sun-Maid, for always being so consistent—something timeless and wonderful in an ever changing fast-paced world.

Jacqueline C.

SHARING SUN-MAID ▼

Sun-Maid raisins are even more fun to eat when you share them with someone you love!

Kyle & Caitlyn K.

SUN-MAID EXCITEMENT ►

My son loves Sun-Maid raisins. He was playing with the box after he had eaten them when I managed to capture his excitement.

Lisa C.

JUST ME AND MY DAD

When I was in grades K-2, we lived in New York City. My dad was a pastor and his schedule was flexible, so he would make our lunches and walk us to school. We didn't have much money then, so whenever I opened my lunch and found a box of raisins, it was always a thrill!

Today, at 35 years old, I got into work to find a package of those amazing little raisins on my chair! My dad stopped here before I got in and left them for me. What a special man and what special memories those little red boxes have for me!

Vickie E.

GRANDMA'S DARK CAKE

When my grandmother came to the United States in the early 1920s, she and Grandpa moved to California. My grandmother continued to make her English recipes from memory for her family. Our favorite was her dark cake, a spicy cake, full of raisins with no eggs and very little shortening. She often told us how this was the only cake she could make in World War I, as she could get the ingredients.

At least daily when grandchildren were staying with her, she opened her pantry to get her big tub of flour and one of the many boxes of Sun-Maid raisins she kept on hand.

Fortunately we persuaded her to write down the recipe and her grandchildren still make it. When I buy Sun-Maid raisins to do so, I can remember how happy and loved I felt in my grandma's kitchen—stirring and licking spoons.

Cynthia R.

RAISIN TREATS AT GRANDMA'S

Wow, I get the warm fuzzies when I look at those little red boxes of raisins! Such great memories! I remember as a little girl going to my Grandma's house. Often my two sisters and I would spend the night or evening there when my parents were out together. We could always count on receiving a little box of our own raisins! They were so yummy and I never worried about getting them stuck in my teeth or causing cavities! We begged Mom to start buying those raisins that Grandma bought, and so when we started to school, yes, they ended up in our lunches quite often. I loved that part of lunch! To this day, I still buy those raisins and often end up eating the whole box by myself! I'm glad that I need iron!

Denise I.

RAISINS AHOY! ▼

When I was younger, raisins were simply the epitome of every snack and best enjoyed while watching cartoons. Not much has changed! I've just outgrown the sailor suit.

Molly W.

THE BOX WHISTLE ▼

My favorite thing about having a box of Sun-Maid raisins in my lunch-box was eating up all the raisins as fast as I could, so that I could use the box as a whistle. While this annoyed my teachers, all the kids I knew also used to do this, so we'd have this impromptu chorus of whistling raisin boxes every day at lunch. Even today, whenever I pack a small box of Sun-Maid raisins for my lunch at work, I sometimes find myself doing the box-whistle thing to remind myself of simpler times in my life…I guess there's some things that never change.

Tony W.

MOM'S SOFT RAISIN COOKIES —A FAMILY LEGACY

It was 1956, the school bus was cold and drafty on the way home and my stomach was churning, as I was ready for my after-school snack. I was looking forward to Mom's soft raisin cookies and hot chocolate milk. They were Dad's favorite cookies too, so Mom made them often. Once I was grown-up and married, Mom's cookie recipe became my husband's favorite and 6 years later we had a son and it wasn't long before her cookies were one of his favorites, too. Years later, my three grandsons enjoyed the raisin cookies and we would make them together. Now, our great-granddaughter is learning to cook and I am passing Mom's soft raisin cookie recipe on to her. Five generations have enjoyed Mom's recipe. Where did she get it? I don't know, but I wouldn't be surprised if it was from Sun-Maid.

Mary Jane L.

HOPE FOR A SAFE FUTURE

My memory isn't really a memory, but rather a hope for a safe future. Your Sun-Maid Mini-Snacks are the perfect gift for shipping overseas. My husband has a nephew stationed in Afghanistan—sometimes out in the mountains at 7,000 feet where, of course, it's very cold. We send him "care boxes" with snack items that he can take with him while he is on a mission out of camp, for several days at a time. These packages must withstand the extreme heat and extreme cold, and raisins are the perfect answer.

Thanks for assisting in creating "care boxes" that will create a pleasant memory amid the unpleasant ones that he experiences.

Gloria

THAT WASN'T CANDY?

When visiting my grandmother she would always let us go to the pantry and find ourselves a snack. Opening the doors I would instantly grab up

one of those little red boxes thinking my grandma was great for giving me candy. She would just smile. To this day I still buy those little boxes and it still feels like that special treat my grandma would keep just for me.

Donna M.

ALWAYS IN THE PANTRY

Gradually, the number of my siblings around the kitchen table grew to nine. Need I have to say, Mom thought carefully about what was healthy for us to eat. It was in the Depression years. Your raisins were in our cereal, pies, rice pudding, cakes, and cookies. We loved everything even though my brothers would say, "Raisins again? Mom, if a box of raisins was not in this house, you would not know how to cook!"

I am now 84, old habits are hard to break, and at home there are raisins, raisins, everywhere. If it isn't Sun-Maid, it isn't there.

Mary G.

MY GRANDDAUGHTER ▼

Sun-Maid raisins are my granddaughter Madison's favorite snack. She and Pappy sit for hours on the porch talking and nibbling every weekend.

Debra L.

SWEET DREAMS ►

A picture is worth a thousand words.

Brooke K.

GRANDMA'S FAVORITE SNACKS

My maternal grandma's favorite snack was classic Sun-Maid raisins. Whenever my uncle from California visited us, he would have boxes and boxes of Sun-Maid raisins for my grandma. I also continue with that tradition of bringing Sun-Maid raisins to my grandma whenever I return home from studying at college in California.

During my grandma's funeral service, I bought along boxes of Sun-Maid raisins for her as part of the offerings. In our culture, we burn offerings as a gesture of sending those important and favorite items of our loved ones. That way she would be able to use those items on her journey in the other world.

Sun-Maid raisins remind me of my grandma all the time because that was the only brand of raisins she would eat as snacks with us growing up.

M. Chui

DADDY'S FAVORITE PIE

When I was growing up my family never ate many sweets or desserts. We would just eat those little boxes of raisins because they were good. If I had realized how nutritious they were, my brother and I might not have eaten them. All of the kids in the neighborhood loved those little boxes of raisins. My Mama would always make the usual pecan pie, pumpkin pie, and other desserts on holidays. I do remember her making Daddy a raisin pie a lot. He absolutely loved raisin pie.

I never eat or cook with raisins without remembering how much my Daddy loved those raisin pies, but I guess we all did. This makes me want to make a raisin pie but better yet see if my Mama would make me one. My family still loves to eat raisins. Thank you Sun-Maid for your great raisins.

Mary Ann W.

CUTTING BOARD COMMUNICATION ▼

One evening my husband and I watched the grandkids for a few hours. I made sandwiches for them to eat, using raisins to make faces on the sandwiches. Our granddaughter ate her raisins right up and I gave her some more.

Later, she followed me into the kitchen and was trying to tell me what she wanted (she's almost two).

Without pausing, she walked over to the cutting boards we have leaning up against the wall, pulled forward the first two and pointed to the Sun-Maid cutting board that a friend had given me a year or so before. She knows her logos. And she got her raisins.

Julie M.

IT STARTED WITH GRANDMA

The thought of Grandma's mincemeat full of Sun-Maid raisins, currants, and muscats is a happy memory. I remember helping her to mix it in her big granite washtub, and the aroma of each box of Sun-Maid raisins, the currants and the muscats so moist and chewy, all going in one by one to make the base of her old-fashioned treat. Grinding the fresh-from-the-orchard apples and the citron, along with the beef was a true labor of love. But the smells all came together with the spices, the molasses stirred in, and it was at last mincemeat. We canned it into hot jars for 4 weeks or so and then waited until it could be used in the star pie for Thanksgiving. Grandma wanted to share for generations her amazing treat, and we still look forward to making it and sharing it with family and friends. Thanks to Sun-Maid, they are the best!

Paula N.

RAISIN THE PAST ▼

I remember eating Sun-Maid raisins in my parents' backyard while reading Hardy Boys books under a *Pennantia baylisiana* tree (the rarest tree in the world). Sun-Maid raisins bring me back to a time when a pack of gum cost a nickel and life was simple.

Sam S.

CALIFORNIA SUNSHINE IN BROOKLYN, NEW YORK ▲

Thank you for bringing a moment of joy to the steps of Brooklyn. Now our son is showing his little sister how to follow in his footsteps.

Jamison & Eleanor K.

HOOKY COOKIES

About once a year my mom would let me be too "sick" to go to school. It was an unspoken agreement that we would have a day together. An inside day. No friends, no dad, no brother, just me and my mommy.

We always ended up in the kitchen making oatmeal cookies. My job was to measure and add the ingredients… and to spoon the cookies onto the sheet. She did the mixing, chopped the walnuts, and baked the cookies.

The last thing to go in the mixing bowl was the Sun-Maid raisins. They went in last so they didn't get mashed from too much mixing. I can still remember the wonderful smells from those cookies baking. The brown sugar, the vanilla, and, of course, the raisins! Mom is gone now, but those memories will be with me forever.

Tom B.

A LESSON IN RAISINS ▶

I remember doing a report on raisins for fourth grade. I researched raisins from our school library and used all the different ways in 1970 to access information about raisins. There were no accessible computers at that time. To finish off my report, I had my parents purchase the little boxes of raisins, enough to feed the entire class. I distributed the little boxes while reading my report. It was one of the best reports the class had experienced that year. I believe it was thanks to the Sun-Maid raisins that I provided.

After the report, I remember having Sun-Maid raisins in the little box for snack time. As a family, we didn't receive cookies or chips as snacks. And the most convenient and fun snack choice was Sun-Maid raisins. My parents had decided, from my report, that raisins were the best choice for our family to enjoy at snack time.

Donna S.

A SNACK AND A SMOOCH ▼

I remember always carrying around the little red boxes of raisins when I was small. They were the perfect size. Now, I toss them in all my bags to have ready for my sons. On the day of this photo, my son, Cole, shared his raisins, and a sunny smooch, with his friend, Caroline.

Kate C.

CHAPTER 4

From Field to Table

Planting a Raisin Vineyard

A raisin vineyard is a long-term investment. Not only is it hard work, but it takes 3 years for a new vine to bear fruit that is commercially viable. If the vines are well-tended, they can produce fruit for 100 years or more. The type of grape bears consideration as well. There are many varieties, but most raisin growers still prefer the Thompson Seedless type, which constitutes 95 percent of the Fresno area raisin crops.

PREPARING THE SITE

Before grapes are planted, the ground is leveled to insure proper irrigation. Leveling occurs while the soil is dry. Wet soil would compact, making root and water penetration difficult. Most raisin vineyards are planted in rows that run from East to West to optimize sun exposure in the middle of the rows and to maximize the sun's drying potential at harvest.

PLANTING AND PRUNING

Traditionally, vineyards are planted with dormant rootings or cuttings. Vines are rarely trained in the first year, but allowed to grow for maximum leaf area, which facilitates root system development and carbohydrate production through photosynthesis.

TRAINING

Training grapevines up the stake and across a trellis is a key component of viticulture. Careful management of the vine canopy ensures proper balance between shade and sun. There must be enough foliage for adequate photosynthesis. Too much foliage can over-shade plants, slowing down the ripening process, and it can also cause some vine diseases.

CHOOSING THE RIGHT LOCATION

Climate, soil, and water are the main considerations when planting a vineyard. The San Joaquin Valley has optimum weather, contains well-drained sandy loam soil, and enjoys hot, dry Septembers that allow grapes to reach optimal sweetness. The Coast Ranges to the west create a basin of fog in the winter, allowing fruit crops to rest in dormancy, saving their energy for vigorous spring growth.

CONVENTIONAL TRELLIS

The first trellis system simply tied canes upright to a stake in the ground. In the 1890s, growers began stretching horizontal wires between stakes to support the new shoots. A cross arm was added to widen the trellis in the 1940s, which let in more sun and thus improved size and sugar content.

OVERHEAD TRELLIS

Many trellis systems have been developed to improve production of different grape varieties, and to allow specialized harvesting equipment to move through the vines. The overhead trellis system trains vines up onto wires stretched 6½ feet overhead. Grapes hang from the canopy for easy access during harvest.

OPEN GABLE TRELLIS

The open gable trellis connects trellis wires between rows of 6-foot high V-shaped supports. The unique V shape lets in plenty of sunlight and focuses, or traps, the heat. This greatly improves photosynthesis, ripening, and drying. Workers can easily walk under this type of trellis and access fruit and canes for hand operations.

THE MIGHTY VALLEY

Anyone who drives along California Highway 99 will pass through perfect raisin-growing country. In the San Joaquin Valley, annual production is more than 350,000 tons, which accounts for much of the world's raisin supply. This is thanks to the area's natural resources and dedicated growers.

The Cycle of Grape Growing

The cycle of grape growing begins each winter when the grapevines are dormant. During December and January, the vines are pruned to regulate the next summer's production. The major growth stages thereafter are budbreak, bloom (or flowering), berry set, veraison (berry softening and initiation of color development), fruit maturity (summer/early fall harvest), and then the cycle beginning again with dormancy (late fall/winter rest).

APRIL

Budbreak occurs in March when miniature shoots begin to appear. In April, tender bunches form on the shoots. By routinely counting the bunches each year, growers are provided with the first estimate of the potential size of the summer crop.

MAY

In May, the bunches are in bloom. There is a tiny flower for every grape on the bunch. Fortunately, grapes are hermaphroditic and can pollinate themselves, without the need for bees. Once pollinated, a small seed trace forms and the grape begins to grow around it. Irrigation becomes critical at this time to keep the crop growing. By the end of May, berry set begins.

JUNE

In June, the grapes continue to grow toward maturity. In addition to irrigation and disease prevention, growers monitor for potential insect infestations. Growers must be able to identify the pest, the damage it does, and determine if there are sufficient beneficial insects to control the problem. Armed with this information, the grower can make the best decision for the crop and the environment.

JULY

Irrigation is most critical in July, as the temperature on many days exceeds 100°F (38°C). Proper irrigation will prevent vine stress and maximize the size of the crop. The week of July 4th is the beginning of the grapes developing fruit sugar, lowering acid, and becoming soft. This stage is called *veraison*. Veraison is the French term for ripening.

AUGUST

At the beginning of August, growers stop irrigating the vines to dry the soil in preparation for harvest. From the last week in August to the first week in September, Thompson Seedless grapes are plump, ripe, and ready for harvest. Generally, it takes 4$\frac{1}{2}$ pounds of grapes to make 1 pound of raisins. After the first frost, usually in November, the leaves turn orange and brittle and fall to the ground, telling the grower his vineyard is ready for pruning and the start of a new season.

Hand Harvesting

The traditional and primary practice of using field labor to hand harvest grapes into natural sun-dried raisins is much the same today as it was 100 years ago. Irrigation is stopped in August to dry the soil. Before harvest, growers terrace the soil to make it smooth, firm, and sloping south to maximize sun exposure. When grapes reach the peak of sweetness, they are hand cut from the vine and spread onto individual paper trays (generally 24 x 36 inches, 0.6 x 0.9 meters). Temperatures on the trays can reach 120 to 140°F (50 to 62°C).

1. PICKING THE BUNCHES

Hand laborers cut each bunch from the vine using a curve-tipped knife. The grape bunch is held while being cut from the stem. Hand harvesting minimizes grape damage.

2. GRAPE PANS

The freshly cut grape bunches are then placed into plastic grape pans that hold between 18 and 22 pounds of grapes when full. A full grape pan will fill one paper tray.

3. SPREADING THE GRAPES TO DRY

The picker places the grape bunches onto the paper tray and spreads them evenly to cover the entire tray. The paper trays are placed side by side facing south to maximize drying time and sun exposure. Most vineyard rows are either ⅛ mile or ¼ mile long.

4. SOLAR DRYING

Many people are surprised to learn that Thompson Seedless grapes are green or amber green at harvest. The southern San Joaquin Valley is an ideal area to dry grapes into dark brown raisins because of its long, hot, and dry summers, which continue into early fall.

5. SUN-DRIED

The grapes will lie on the trays for 17 to 21 days and turn into raisins. When the raisins are almost dry, the paper tray is rolled into a roll. This roll acts like a solar oven, both finishing the drying process and allowing the raisin moisture to equalize. The drying is complete when the raisins reach 10 to 14 percent moisture.

THOMPSON TRADITION

Since the 1920s, most grapes planted for hand harvesting are of the Thompson Seedless variety, because of their sweet flavor and lack of seeds. Thompsons replaced the Muscat variety, which became less preferred by consumers because of its seeds.

READY FOR PICKING

Grapes are harvested when grape sugars reach between 18° to 22° Brix. The higher the grape sugar, the higher the yield. Grapes harvested at 18° Brix have a drying ratio of 4.63:1, while 22° Brix grapes have a drying ratio of 3.74:1.

FINISHED HARVESTING

In this photo circa 1960, a worker picks the rolls from the field and empties these into wooden "sweat boxes." These smaller sweatboxes have been replaced with wooden bins which typically hold 1,000 pounds (500 kg) of raisins.

Mechanical Harvesting

California industry efforts for mechanical raisin harvesting and field drying began in earnest in the early 1970s. However, widespread use of these techniques did not occur until the 1990s. Today, 25 percent of California's annual sun-dried raisin crop is mechanically harvested onto continuous paper trays in the field.

1. HARVEST CANE CUTTING

Harvest cane cutting is the process of cutting the cane by hand between the bunch and the vine at least 10 days prior to harvesting. Cutting the canes allows the capstem on the berries to dry and become brittle. After 10 days of drying, the berries require less force to remove, which improves the entire harvesting process and makes a better raisin.

2. MACHINE HARVESTING

Two machines move together down parallel rows in the vineyard. The mechanical harvester and the tray layer work together in sequence to harvest grapes from the vine and lay these evenly onto a long, continuous roll of paper.

3. OVER THE ROW CONVEYER

When the grapes are shaken from the vine by the machine harvester, they are conveyed over the vine row to the tray layer and placed in the tray layer hopper.

4. PAPER TRAY LAYER

The tray layer hopper spreads the grapes evenly, one or two grapes thick, onto a continuous paper tray for even and faster drying. The continuous paper tray typically runs the entire length of the row, usually a quarter mile or longer (approximately 430 meters).

5. SUNSHINE

The drying time for raisins mechanically harvested onto a continuous tray is 7 to 10 days. This is approximately 10 days faster than hand harvested raisins and is the result of drying individual grapes instead of grape bunches.

6. PICKUP

When the grapes have dried into raisins, a machine picks up the raisins from the continuous tray, transfers the raisins into bins in the next row, and shreds the paper tray so it can be incorporated into the soil.

7. HARVEST COMPLETE

A tractor pulling a bin trailer loaded with bins travels at the same speed as the machine harvester and completes the harvest. Once in the bin, the raisins travel on to the processing and packaging plant.

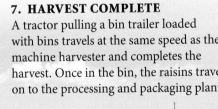

Dried-on-the-Vine Harvesting

Raisins dry much slower on the vine than on paper trays laid on the ground. Dried-on-the-vine research began in Australia in the late 1950s and early 1960s. The most significant development of this early research was the practice of cutting the canes upon fruit maturity, before taking the grapes off the vine. With the advent of earlier ripening raisin grape types, Fiesta, DOVine, and Selma Pete, California growers expanded early experimental production to become a viable part of the raisin industry by the first years of the 21st century.

HARVEST CANE CUTTING

Cutting the canes by hand between the bunch and the vine initiates the drying process. Once the canes are cut, the bunches will become raisins in 6 to 8 weeks.

OPEN GABLE TRELLIS

An open gable trellis is a large V-shaped structure supported on top of a metal stake. The V-shaped structures are connected by wires which run the length of the row. The rows are 11 to 12 feet apart, which leaves an opening between the trellis structures. This system allows for ample sunlight and makes it easier for workers to perform their work.

OPEN GABLE HARVEST

With earlier ripening grape varieties, canes are cut by hand by mid-August, allowing the bunches to then begin to dry. When the bunches have dried into raisins, they can be harvested with a wine grape harvester that has been modified to place the raisins in bins instead of gondolas.

OVERHEAD TRELLIS

The overhead trellis system is made up of a series of wires that run both directions about 6½ feet off the ground. The fruit grows in one row and the canes, which will produce next year's crop, grow in the next row. This pattern is repeated across the entire field. Workers have easy access to perform their work. Because of the expansive leaf foliage and increased photosynthesis, this system produces the highest yields per acre.

OVERHEAD TRELLIS HARVESTING

Canes are cut by hand by mid-August, allowing the bunches to dry. When the bunches have dried into raisins, they can be harvested by machine harvesters that drive under the vines and vibrate them off into bins. While this is done, vacuums remove dried leaves from the raisins.

DOV SUCCESS

After years of effort, growers and industry partners have successfully developed an entirely new drying method and new varieties to enhance them. DOV production has become a significant contributor to the California raisin industry. With higher yields, lower costs, and lower labor needs, DOV truly is a raisin technique for the future.

Sustainable Farming & Processing

Raisins are the natural product of grapes and sunshine, and have been produced using sustainable methods long before "green" became a popular buzzword. Sun-Maid's organic raisins are just the beginning of the company's efforts to promote sustainable farming and processing.

PRODUCED
WITH SOLAR ENERGY

During the summer months, the San Joaquin Valley's hot summer days help ripen the grapes. When it's time for drying the grapes into raisins, both the sun and the heated soil work together like an oven to transform the grapes into raisins. Solar energy dries about 2.5 billion pounds of fresh grapes, which saves the equivalent of 600 trillion British thermal units (BTU) of natural gas each year. With 548,000 miles of grapevines in California, that's enough to circle the Earth 22 times.

RECYCLED PAPER

Raisins are dried by the sun in the vineyard atop large sheets of paper called paper trays. After harvest, the paper trays are collected and recycled.

WATER WISE
At the Sun-Maid plant, water used in the raisin-cleaning process is reused to irrigate forage for cattle.

EVERYTHING PUT TO USE
Even capstems and stems removed during raisin processing are sold for cattle feed.

SUSTAINABLE PACKAGING
Raisin packages are shipped in corrugated cartons made from trees grown in sustainable forests, marked with the Sustainable Forestry Initiative label. Recycled material is used in outer packaging and all inks are water-based.

PUTTING THE GRAPE TO GOOD USE
At Sun-Maid's distillery facility (*below*), raisins are turned into high-proof alcohol utilized in brandy and white wine. Effluent water from the still is sent to a methane digester at the distillery facility (*right*). The digester generates energy—a sustainable replacement for natural gas—which is used to operate the distillery's boiler.

Hazards of Raisin Growing

Even in the world's most ideal raisin-producing region, Mother Nature continues to dictate success or disaster. Raisin growers must mitigate hazards including ill-timed weather and severe temperatures in order to produce naturally sun-dried raisins. Because the majority of California raisins are sun-dried on paper trays laid out on the terraced soil beside the vines, rain during the drying phase represents the biggest threat to the raisin crop.

An Analysis:

THE FROST OF 1972
PETE CHRISTENSEN
FRESNO COUNTY FARM ADVISOR

FROST

A severe spring freeze on March 27 and 28 spelled disaster for the 1972 raisin crop, resulting in the smallest raisin crop in 75 years.

RAIN

In 1976, disastrous September rains destroyed nearly half of the industry's crop. Again, in September 1978, nearly 70 percent of the drying raisins were lost to rain.

RIPENING SCHEDULE

Thompson Seedless grapes ripen late in the season, putting growers at greater risk of rain damage. The development of varieties including Fiesta, DOVine, and Selma Pete—which ripen earlier in the month—has helped growers to complete harvest earlier.

Ripening Schedule — AUGUST

SUN	MON	TUE	WED	THU	FRI	SAT
			1	2	3	4
						Selma Pete
5	6	7	8	9	10	11
Selma Pete				DOVine and Zante Currant		
12	13	14	15	16	17	18
DOVine and Zante Currant						Fiesta
19	20	21	22	23	24	25
Fiesta					Thompson Seedless	
26	27	28	29	30	31	1
Thompson Seedless						

DRYING CALENDAR

The California raisin harvest usually begins in the first part of September. During ideal hot and dry climate conditions, Thompson Seedless grapes dry into raisins in 17 to 21 days.

Drying Calendar

SEPTEMBER

SUN	MON	TUE	WED	THU	FRI	SAT
2	3	4	5	6	7	8
9	10	11	12	13	14 **Trays Turned**	15
16	17	18	19	20	21	22
23	24	25	26	27	28	29
						30

SPRING

Spring frosts below 31°F (-0.6°C) can damage the grapevine's young shoots and flower clusters. Hail in springtime can also damage shoots and clusters.

SUMMER

Cool temperatures or moist conditions can delay maturity of the crop. Excessive heat can also burn the vine and the clusters, causing damage.

FALL

Rain during harvest can cause damage to the raisins. Long periods of rainy weather can cause crop loss in the field.

Sun-Maid Experts

It takes people with a wide variety of skills and expertise to bring raisins from the vineyard to the packing house and consumer. The process begins with Sun-Maid growers, whose experience growing grapes and drying them into raisins is the first step toward making the World's Favorite Raisin™. After the raisins have been delivered to Sun-Maid's facility from the growers, they are stored safely until they are ready to be packaged. Inside the plant, machine operators oversee the inspection, processing, and packaging of all Sun-Maid products.

GRAPE SUGAR
Sun-Maid grower Jeff Bortolussi uses a refractometer to check grape sugar levels prior to harvest. Growers monitor their grapes and the weather conditions closely to choose the best time to harvest.

HEALTHY VINES
In his dried-on-the-vine overhead vineyard, Sun-Maid grower Steve Kister uses a hand lens to inspect a grape leaf. Kister converted his vineyard operations to an overhead trellis system, increasing his productivity per acre and enabling the use of mechanical harvesting methods.

RAISIN STACK
Each year, growers deliver 100,000 tons of raisins to Sun-Maid's Kingsburg headquarters. Once the raisins have been inspected, they are stored in 1,000-pound wooden bins. The skilled crew stacks and covers the bins. The raisins remain in storage until they are ready to be processed and packaged.

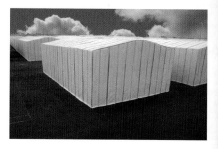

GROWERS' FIELD DAY
Field days and seminars are key to keeping Sun-Maid growers up to date with all phases of raisin production.

QUALITY CHECKS
A Sun-Maid laboratory technician continually tests samples from the production line for quality.

DOWN THE LINE
A packaging supervisor inspects finished cartons, which are about to be packed into cases.

GOLDEN STANDARD
Boxes of golden raisins travel down the line after being filled. Sun-Maid operates the largest raisin packaging facility in the world and has led the industry in specialized equipment for processing raisins.

California's Raisin Pioneers

The story of the Sun-Maid grower begins with immigration, as California pioneers settled and shaped a land full of opportunities. Germans from Russia, Japanese-Americans, Italians, Danes, Swedes, Mexicans, Yugoslavs, Sikhs, and Portuguese are among the many ethnic groups that have been part of the California raisin industry's international melting pot.

Most closely associated with raisins are the Armenians, who helped to originate the crop in Persia between 120 and 900 A.D. and are still among the world's greatest viticulturists. They began arriving in Fresno County in the 1890s, and quickly became known within the dried-fruit industry as growers and, eventually, packers.

Like so many people who carved out new lives here, the Armenians loved the land. One Tulare County community they established was named Yettem—an Armenian word for paradise or Garden of Eden.

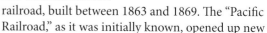

COMING TO AMERICA
New York's Statue of Liberty greeted many immigrants who arrived in the United States through Ellis Island between 1892 and 1954. Helping connect the east side of the country with the west was the world's first transcontinental railroad, built between 1863 and 1869. The "Pacific Railroad," as it was initially known, opened up new markets for products that could be shipped across country and brought immigrants west. When California became a state in 1850, its first census recorded a population of only 92,597.

Today, California has the greatest population of any state in the United States with over 37 million people.

JAPANESE-AMERICAN GROWERS

Sun-Maid's grower membership has always consisted of a variety of ethnic groups, and Japanese-American raisin growers were no exception. This photograph of the Nakamura vineyard was taken in 1924. Nearly two decades later, thousands of American citizens of Japanese descent were forced into internment following an executive order issued by President Franklin D. Roosevelt after the attack on Pearl Harbor. While many Japanese-American landowners throughout the Western U.S. lost all their property, many Sun-Maid growers maintained their neighbors' properties while they were away, illustrating the principles of cooperation at the heart of the organization.

FOUR GENERATIONS OF FARMING

(*Left*) Sun-Maid grower Jon Marthedal, pictured with his son, Eric, is a third-generation California raisin grower, continuing the tradition his farming ancestors began in Denmark dating back to the 1500s. Marthedal's grandfather came to Fresno County in 1903, and began growing diversified crops including grapes, cotton, and corn.

FAMILY FARM

(*Right*) Jon Marthedal's mother is pictured with her brothers and sisters on the family farm. Jon Marthedal knew, after successfully growing his own raisins on a rented vineyard as a high school junior, that farming would also be his profession. He continues to grow raisins, tree fruit, and blueberries.

PASSING ON WISDOM & TRADITION

(*Left*) Eric Marthedal as a child with his grandfather, Harold Marthedal. Eric Marthedal now continues the farming tradition.

California Population Growth: Waves of Immigration

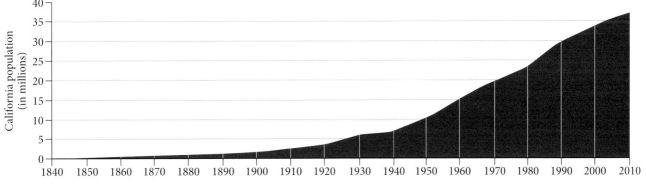

Gold Rush (1848–1869)	Land Boom (1886–1888)	Rise of the Automobile and Agricultural Growth (1914–1929)	Manufacturing and Industry (1941–1945)	Postwar Boom— Agriculture and Industry (1948–1970)	Economic Recovery and Recession (1982–1989)	Melting Pot (2004)
Immigration mostly from East Coast, Midwest, and western Europe	Principally in Southern California, immigrants from within the U.S.	Boom from the end of World War I to the beginning of the Great Depression	Post-Depression boom spurred by World War II. Immigrants from within the U.S. and larger groups of African Americans and Latinos	Immigrants from within the U.S. and Latin America, Asia, and Western Europe	Influxes from Asia and Latin America	California achieves a statewide "minority majority," with no ethnic group constituting a majority

Processing & Packaging

Natural seedless raisins are dried by the sun and travel from the field directly to Sun-Maid headquarters, where they are processed and packaged before being shipped to consumers around the world.

RAISINS ARRIVE
Raisins come to Sun-Maid's warehouses in their natural condition from the field.

PROCESSING BEGINS
Bins of raisins are emptied onto the processing line. Specialized equipment removes the coarse vine stems from the raisins and cap stems are removed from the raisins by machines called cappers.

WATER BATH
Raisins are washed with water until they are thoroughly cleaned.

LASER SORTER
Laser sorters remove stems and other foreign materials with precision accuracy.

TO THE PACKAGING LINES
From processing, raisins move to
25 packaging lines.

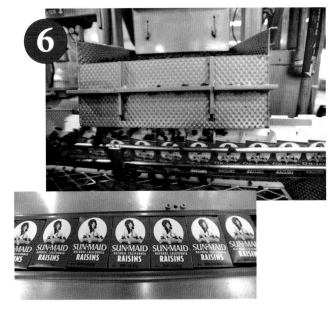

PACKAGES ARE FILLED
Raisins are filled into numerous sized packs,
from ½ ounce/15 gram Mini-Snacks® to
1,000 pound/500kg totes.

DOWN THE LINE
Once filled and sealed, packages are
conveyed to be placed into cases.

READY TO GO
Cases are assembled onto pallets
and stored until shipped.

Distribution in the United States

Back in the early 20th century, Sun-Maid raisins traveled across the country by train shipments. At times these trains were loaded with thousands of tons of raisins and the rail cars featured signs proclaiming "Raisins Grown by 6,000 California Growers."

In 1915, the "Sun-Maid Special" traveled to Chicago in record time to deliver raisins for the annual Raisin Day celebration when restaurants across the country featured raisin-themed dishes on their menus. These raisin trains helped to create a demand for raisins outside California, where consumers previously had limited access to raisins.

Today, people all over the U.S. can purchase raisins with ease, thanks to streamlined customer and supply chain services. Coordinated efforts between customer service, transportation, warehouse administration, and demand planning departments deliver Sun-Maid's entire line of dried fruit to store shelves and food manufacturers.

Sales are divided between retail, in which consumers purchase Sun-Maid products at stores, and bulk, in which food manufacturers purchase Sun-Maid products for use in their own food items.

RAISINS BY RAIL

When the Sun-Maid processing facility was opened in 1918, railroads were the primary means for distribution. Today, delivery of Sun-Maid products across the U.S. is done by truck and rail.

SOUTHERN PACIFIC

This 1925 photograph (*left*) shows boxes of raisins being loaded by hand directly from the Sun-Maid plant onto a Southern Pacific railcar.

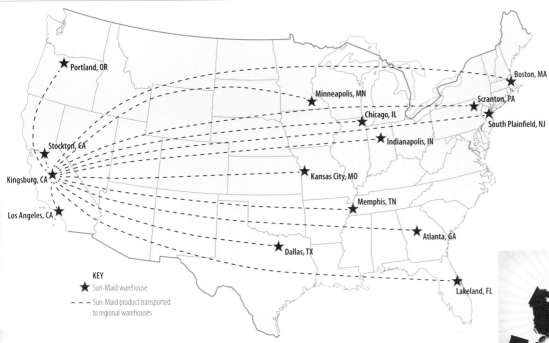

MAKING THEIR WAY

A network of warehouses enable Sun-Maid products to reach both retail and industrial customers, who buy dried fruits for use in products including cereals and baked goods.

INTERNATIONAL TRAVEL

Sun-Maid products travel from Kingsburg, California to their final destinations across the U.S., Canada, and to more than 50 countries throughout the world.

LOCAL DELIVERY

Sun-Maid works with a number of regional warehousing and logistics firms to provide prompt local deliveries. One of these is Kane, of Scranton, Pennsylvania.

READY TO SHIP

Pallets of Sun-Maid products are stacked and ready for shipment.

ALL IN THE FAMILY

Kane recently celebrated its 80th anniversary. The company has been family-owned for the past four generations. This photograph (*above*) is of the present Kane family management.

Distribution Around the World

While the grapes for Sun-Maid's raisins all come from a 50-mile radius around Fresno, California, the finished products are sold in more than 50 countries around the world. Getting the packaged dried fruit to these destinations involves a coordinated effort between several departments at Sun-Maid, along with shippers, distributors, and brokers.

Most international orders are packed to order, which means they are stored until they are ready to be packaged and shipped. Pallets of dried fruit are loaded onto trailers, which are transported by truck to shipping ports in Oakland and Long Beach, California. Shipments to Europe are transported to Houston, Texas on trains and then shipped overseas in container ships.

INTERNATIONAL OPERATIONS
Shipping clerks coordinate the logistics of overseas raisin deliveries from Sun-Maid's Fresno plant, circa 1925.

California, USA

Guatemala

Mexico

Washington, D.C., USA

Brazil

AROUND THE WORLD WITH SUN-MAID
Sun-Maid products are sold in more than 50 countries worldwide, and the company is continually looking to expand the distribution of its raisins and dried fruits to make them more available to consumers.

El Salvador

Colombia

Canada

Honduras

Ecuador

Cuba

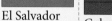

Iceland

Nicaragua

Panama

Bahamas

DEVASTATING EARTHQUAKE & TSUNAMI

JAPAN EARTHQUAKE 2011
Natural disasters like the Japanese earthquake and tsunami of 2011 can interrupt and affect distribution.

Peru

TRANSPORT TO HAMBURG
Boxes of Sun-Maid raisins travel through Hamburg, Germany, in this photo from the early 1900s.

Venezuela

SUN-MAID SHIPMENT

Sun-Maid products are ready to be transported from truck to ship in this 1963 photo.

ACROSS THE SEAS

Huge container ships transport Sun-Maid products from Oakland, California, to destinations across the globe.

Ireland

Norway

France

Finland

Russian Federation

Vietnam

China

Japan

United Kingdom

Sweden

Czech Republic

Latvia

Oman

Thailand

Mongolia

South Korea

Denmark

Egypt

Israel

United Arab Emirates

Cambodia

Singapore

Australia

Netherlands

South Africa

Bahrain

Indonesia

Taiwan

New Zealand

Poland

Saudi Arabia

Brunei Darussalam

Germany

Qatar

India

Philippines

French Polynesia

Sri Lanka

Malaysia

8 kostråd

Eating Well with Canada's Food Guide

Canada

El Pla

CEREALES

The food circle

Something from each group everyday

5층
유지, 견과 및

4층
우유 및 유제

3층
고기, 생선

2층
채소류 | 고

1층
곡류 및

The Facts on Raisins & Dried Fruits

Choosing Raisins

For nearly 100 years, the most popular grape used for making raisins has been the Thompson Seedless grape—which, like the seedless watermelon, has no seeds. What makes natural raisins "natural" is that they are sun-dried without any oils or dipping solutions to accelerate their drying. Natural seedless raisins have a sweet, chewy, and rich flavor enjoyed by children and adults alike.

NATURAL SEEDLESS RAISINS

About 90 to 95 percent of natural seedless raisins are made from Thompson Seedless varieties, which includes Selma Pete (*shown above*), DOVine, and Fiesta, while the remaining percentage is made up of varieties including Flame Seedless, Ruby Seedless, and Sultana.

ZANTE CURRANTS

Zante currants are made from Black Corinth grapes, a seedless grape variety that originated in Greece. Zante currants are very small, black, tender, and have a tart, spicy flavor. They are only 1 to 2 percent of natural seedless grape production.

BAKING WITH ZANTES

Not to be confused with blackcurrants and redcurrants, which are berries grown on small shrubs, Zante currants are perfect for baking, and are referred to in recipes as "currants."

THOMPSON SEEDLESS

Thompson Seedless is the dominant grape variety grown in California. Thompson Seedless grapes are usually sun-dried on paper trays for a period of between 17 to 21 days.

FIESTA & FLAME

Selma Pete, DOVine, and Fiesta are all Thompson Seedless varieties, while Flame Seedless is a cross between Thompson Seedless and other varieties including Muscat of Alexandria.

ZANTE CURRANT

Also known as Black Corinth, the Zante Currant is used to make small, seedless raisins. Because of its early ripening and quick drying time, Zante Currants can be dried both on paper trays and on the vine.

Thompson Seedless

Thompson Seedless dried on ground

Fiesta   Flame Seedless

Flame dried on ground

Flame dried on the vine

Zante Currant

Zante Currant dried on ground

Zante Currant dried on the vine

Golden Raisins

Many people are surprised to learn that golden raisins are made from the same varieties of grapes used to make natural seedless raisins. On the vine, the grapes are the same green color, but different processing methods and the treatment of sulfur dioxide give golden raisins their bright, golden color. Instead of being dried in the sun, golden raisins are dried inside large dehydrators.

GOLDEN GOODNESS
Golden raisins are used for snacking and in baked or cooked products.

GRAPES FOR GOLDENS
The Fiesta variety, shown above, is among the grape varieties used to make golden raisins, which includes Thompson Seedless, Fiesta, Selma Pete, and DOVine.

INTRODUCTION OF GOLDEN RAISINS
Raisin dehydration in heated air dryers was first devised in the early 20th century, and the light-colored golden bleached raisin was developed in the early 1920s. At right, a Sun-Maid golden raisin carton from 1922.

COOKING WITH GOLDEN RAISINS
Recipes often call for golden raisins because of their light color. Golden raisins and natural seedless raisins can be substituted for each other in recipes, or for more colorful cooking, combined.

Making Golden Raisins

1. FRESH FROM THE VINEYARD

Grapes are hand harvested and transported to the dehydrator in bins.

2. CLEANING AND PREPARATION

Grapes pass through a shaker and vacuum to remove leaves before being dipped in a warm solution. This produces tiny cracks in the grape skins to prepare the grapes to accept sulfur and speed drying.

3. ONTO TRAYS AND INTO SULFUR TUNNELS

The fruit is placed on wood trays stacked on rolling carts, which go inside sulfur tunnels. The grapes are exposed to sulfur dioxide for 6 to 8 hours, preserving their light color—which can range from yellow to light amber.

4. DRYING TUNNELS

The carts are transferred from the sulfur tunnels to the adjacent drying tunnels, where they are dried in temperatures of 145–155°F for 18 to 20 hours.

5. GOLDEN RAISINS

The trays are removed from the drying tunnels and the golden raisins are taken off the trays and put into bins, which then head to the plant for packaging.

Apricots

Apricot trees thrive in Mediterranean climates like California, Turkey, the Middle East, and South Africa. Apricots have been grown in California for two centuries. Spanish explorers are credited with first introducing apricots to California, where they were planted in the gardens of Spanish missions. The yellow-orange fruits were once a delicacy reserved for royalty, but today, dried apricots are a part of everyday cooking, packing both flavor and a wealth of nutritional benefits.

APRICOT HALVES AND WHOLE APRICOTS

California dried apricots (*right*) are dark orange in color and have a tangy-sweet flavor. They are made by slicing fresh apricots in half, removing the pits, and then drying. Mediterranean dried apricots (*left*) have a sweet flavor. They are pitted and dried whole.

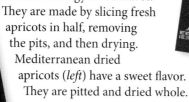

ON THE BRANCH

It takes about 4 years for an apricot tree to begin producing commercial quantities of fruit. Average apricot trees produce fruit for 20 to 25 years. The fruit can be eaten fresh, frozen, canned, or dried. Fresh apricots are generally available from May to August.

MADE IN THE SUN

Trays of halved apricots dry naturally in the sun (*left*). Dried apricots are rich in fiber and other minerals, such as potassium and iron. Apricots also contain beta-carotene, a powerful antioxidant that helps preserve eyesight and is converted into vitamin A by the body.

SWEET AND SAVORY

Dried apricots complement both sweet and savory cooking, in both main dishes and desserts, and their vibrant color adds interest to any table. Here, California dried apricots lend tartness to white chocolate chip cookies (*left*), and Mediterranean dried apricots add sweetness to a North African vegetable stew (*far left*).

APRICOT ABUNDANCE

California's first concentrated area of apricot production was in the Santa Clara Valley, south of San Francisco, which was also known for growing peaches, prunes, plums, and cherries. In the 1970s, the area developed into what is now known as "Silicon Valley," and most of the apricot orchards relocated to the San Joaquin Valley, where they are predominantly found today.

SPRING BLOOMS

The apricot is one of the first fruits to blossom in the spring. It is considered a frost-risk fruit, as it blooms in March so it is easily damaged by the below-freezing temperatures that can occur in April. Apricot production can also be affected by hail, which is unpredictable but occurs in April or May.

APRICOT ORCHARDS

Apricot trees are pruned after harvest. They go into dormancy in winter and begin to develop fruit in February, with the setting of buds. They flower in March or April and are harvested between June and August, depending on variety and location in Northern Hemisphere countries.

Prunes

An ancient fruit originating in Western Asia, prunes were carried westward into Europe, where French cooking has embraced the dried fruit for centuries. As for the United States, prunes were brought to California after the Gold Rush and are now an important part of the state's agriculture. Some people commonly refer to prunes as dried plums.

PLUM ORCHARD

Capable of producing fruit for 30 years, dried plum trees bear fruit 4 to 6 years after planting and reach full production at 8 to 12 years old. After dormancy during the winter months, the trees produce fragrant white blossoms in spring, which last about one week before falling to the ground, revealing the first signs of the forming fruit.

PLUMS TO PRUNES

The D'Agen dried plum is known as the California French Dried Plum and makes up 99 percent of the state's production, which is concentrated in the Sacramento and San Joaquin Valleys. The picture above shows Sun-Maid prune packaging from 1930.

HARVESTING PLUMS

Dried plums are allowed to fully ripen on the tree before being picked for processing, with orchards ready for harvest by mid-August. Most harvesting in California is done by a machine called a mechanical shaker, which grabs a main limb or trunk to shake fruit off the tree onto a fabric-stretched frame. The fruit is transferred into bins by a conveyor belt and then taken to the dehydrator.

PLUM PAST

French nurseryman Louis Pellier originally came to California in 1848 in search of gold, and after little success as a miner, purchased land in the Santa Clara Valley. His brother later joined him and the two began a nursery business with cuttings brought from France, including original D'Agen graft stock brought over in 1856. By 1900, there were approximately 90,000 acres of dried plum orchards in the state. This postcard (*left*) from the early 1900s shows plums being picked by hand before being made into prunes.

PRUNE CUISINE

Far Breton (*near right*), also known as Brittany Pudding, originates from France's northern coastal region. A cross between cake, custard, and flan, the dish calls for prunes and, depending on the region, raisins. A *tagine* (*far right*) is a traditional Moroccan dish, which is named for the clay pot that it is cooked in. Sweet prunes are added to a tagine to balance the flavors of chicken, beef, and lamb.

Figs

The versatile fig grows large and small, round and oval, as a low desert shrub, and towering in tropical forests. Figs may even be the oldest domesticated dried fruit, as they are believed to have been cultivated from as early as 10,000 B.C. Several varieties of figs, including the popular Smyrna variety, were brought to California by settlers and planted in the Sacramento and San Joaquin Valleys. Fresh figs are very perishable. Once dried, figs are easy to transport and can last for months, either to be eaten as snacks or dessert by themselves, or used in baking and other dishes.

CALIMYRNA FIGS

Calimyrna figs require a unique type of pollination by the tiny *Blastophaga* wasp. This process was first successfully completed in California by George Roeding, who hand-pollinated figs brought from Smyrna, Turkey. When the trees produced ripened figs in 1900, he combined the words *Smyrna* and *California* to rename the figs *Calimyrna*.

MISSION FIGS

Mission figs grow in two crops per year. The first crop in late June is used for fresh figs, and the second follows later in the summer, at the same time as many other fig varieties. The second Mission crop is dried for consumer packages of figs and industrially used for fig paste.

COOKING WITH FIGS

Dried figs are rich in health-promoting antioxidants and complex carbohydrates, are an excellent source of dietary fiber, and provide a wealth of essential minerals such as potassium, iron, and calcium. Dried figs make an excellent food for eating out of hand, or using in sweet and savory recipes.

FIG TREES

New plantings of fig trees reach fruit-bearing age after 5 to 7 years, and can produce fruit for 100 years or more. Fruit begins appearing on fig trees in May, and is available as late as October when the final picking of the fruit is completed.

PROCESSING

After the figs have been dried, they are delivered to the processing facility where they are thoroughly washed. Processing brings the moisture content up from 14 to 20 percent when delivered to as high as 31 percent, making the dried figs moist and plump.

FIGS, FORKNER, AND FRESNO

In the early 1900s in Fresno, JC Forkner, third from left, created the world's largest fig orchard. After purchasing land that had been deemed worthless because of a lack of irrigation and hardpan beneath the soil, Forkner bought 48 of the first Fordson tractors ever built to work the soil, later buying even more of the tractors. He spent $8 million developing the land and used dynamite to blast holes to plant over 10,000 acres of figs. He sold 10–40 acre plots and subdivided the acreage closest to Fresno into what would eventually become the "Old Figarden" neighborhood.

FIGS ARE FLOWERS

Unlike other tree fruits or nuts, fig trees have no blossoms on their branches; their flowers are inverted and develop inside the fruit. These tiny flowers produce the small, crunchy seeds that give figs their unique texture.

POSTCARDS

Postcards circa 1914 illustrate fig growing and production in Fresno. In 1890, Fresno County led the state in fig acreage with a total of roughly 3,000 acres, followed by Tulare and Orange counties. By the 1950s, fig planting had grown to roughly 30,000 acres throughout California, led by Fresno, Merced, and Tulare Counties. Today, California fig acreage is roughly 10,000 acres with Madera County leading the state in fig acreage with over 5,000 acres, followed by the counties of Merced and Fresno.

FRUIT AND CAKE

The modern fig bar was invented in 1891, when James Mitchell designed a machine to commercially fill dough with fig jam. The cookies were named for the town of Newton, Massachusetts, which was near Kennedy Biscuit Works (later Nabisco), which first produced the first Fig Newton™ cookies.

Dates

One of the world's first cultivated fruits, dates have long been valued as both a reliable food source and delicacy. People of the Middle East use many varieties, which are classified by ripeness and color, in traditional meals and rituals. Date palms have spread to the New World too, where the dried fruit appears in new guises—from appetizers to desserts.

DELICIOUS DATES
Dates are often stuffed with almonds or other nuts. Dates can be used in meat and rice dishes, as well as baked in desserts. Mature dates have a moisture content of 14 to 22 percent, which is similar to other dried fruits.

DATES IN THE VALLEY
This 1920 photograph shows dates ripening on a tree in Kingsburg, California. Today, most California dates are grown in Southern California's Coachella Valley.

DATE PALMS
While date palm trees (*Phoenix diactylifera*) are grown throughout the world, the trees require special conditions in order to produce fruit. Dates are grown in the Middle East, Pakistan, North America (California and Mexico), and Africa (North of the Sahara, South Africa, and Namibia). Given adequate water, date palms grow in hot, arid climates. Commercial date gardens are made up of male and female trees—the male trees produce pollen and the female trees bear fruit—with one male tree and 50 female trees planted per acre. The trees grow up to 100 feet tall and live more than 200 years.

1. The date garden is prepared for harvest

2. Dates are picked by hand

3. The dates are emptied into bins

DATE HARVEST

Dates ripen in 6 to 7 months and are harvested from September through December in California. In other climates, dates can ripen as early as July and as late as November. Date harvesters either handpick the fruit or cut the ripened clusters and shake off the fruit.

DATE SHAKES

Date shakes are an iconic food of Southern California's Coachella Valley, where the treat originated when date gardens began offering locals and travelers milkshakes made with dates and ice cream.

THE OBSERVANCE OF RAMADAN*

	APRIL	MAY	JUNE	JULY	AUGUST
2012				July 20–Aug. 18	
2013				July 9–Aug. 7	
2014			June 28–July 27		
2015			June 18–July 17		
2016			June 6–July 5		
2017		May 27–June 25			
2018		May 16–June 14			
2019		May 6–June 4			
2020	April 24–May 23				

*Actual timing is dependent on the sighting of the moon.

The ninth month of the Islamic calendar, Ramadan, lasts between 29 and 30 days and is observed by Muslims around the world. During this month, Muslims fast from dawn to sunset. This means that during daylight hours, they cannot consume food or drink, including water. The daily fast is broken by a light meal called *iftar*, usually consisting of dates and water, followed by evening prayers and the offering of a light meal afterwards. The Islamic calendar is based on the moon and has 12 months, alternately 30 and 29 days long. Because the year has 354 days, the dates for Ramadan shift backwards, completing an entire cycle every 32½ years.

Peaches, Apples, & Pears

The flavors of summer and fall last year-round with dried peaches, apples, and pears—traditional dried fruits have nothing added except the treatment of sulfur dioxide for color preservation. While drying concentrates the natural fruit sugars and makes them ideal for snacking and cooking, no sugar or fruit juice concentrates are added, making them an excellent source of essential nutrients including fiber and potassium.

DRYING PEACHES NEAR FRESNO, CALIFORNIA.

A PEACH OF A POSTCARD
Fresno County's first commercially-producing fruit trees were planted in 1877. In 1886, tree fruit began a period of enormous growth, displacing the grain crops that were previously grown in the area.

AUTUMN IN THE ORCHARD
A peach orchard's bright fall colors contrast sharply with the pastel-colored blossoms in spring. Between spring and fall, peak harvest time for peaches runs from June to August, depending on the variety.

DRYING PEACHES
Above, peaches are typically cut in half and the pit is removed before drying. While peaches and nectarines are regarded commercially as different fruits, they belong to the same species. Nectarines have smooth skin, which can often appear more reddish than the skin of fuzzy peaches.

PEACH PACKAGING
Left: Sun-Maid used the Blue Ribbon label to sell peaches before expanding its Sun-Maid product line. *Right*: a man displays peaches drying in the sun at the Earl Fruit Company circa 1930.

APPLES

While there are more than 7,500 varieties of apples worldwide, one of the most popular is the Red Delicious. The Fuji apple variety was introduced to the United States from Japan in the 1980s and is a cross between a Red Delicious and Ralls Janet. Sun-Maid's Dried Washington Apples are made from the popular Fuji variety, which is harvested in October.

BLOSSOM TRAIL

Today, both the Fresno County Fruit Trail and Blossom Trail showcase the vast array of fruits grown in the region, producing maps to guide visitors through the different orchards and vineyards, where the different colored blossoms of plums (white), apricots (pink), peaches and nectarines (both pink and red petals in bloom at the same time), and apples (white) can be seen.

PEARS

Pear harvest begins in August with Bartlett pears and continues in September and October with winter varieties. Both pears and apples are also cut in halves or slices and their seeds are removed before drying. Members of the same subfamily of trees, pears and apples are similar in cultivation, propagation, and pollination.

Artificially Sweetened Dried Fruits

While traditional dried fruits such as apricots, apples, dates, figs, prunes, and raisins have no added sugar, the characteristics of some other fruits make them palatable only when fruit juice or sugar is added to them. Fruits such as blueberries, cherries, cranberries, mangoes, pineapple, papaya, and cantaloupe are all artificially sweetened, and therefore recognized as being different from traditional dried fruits.

CRANBERRIES

Cranberries are one of the few fruits native to North America. They grow on vines in sandy bogs and marshes, and are harvested by flooding the bogs with water so that the cranberries float to the top.

CHERRIES

Cherries have a short harvest season, so drying cherries allows the fruit to be used throughout the year. Sun-Maid's dried cherries are from Northern Michigan, one of the premier areas in the world for tart cherry production.

BLUEBERRIES

Blueberries are also native to North America. Native Americans picked blueberries from bushes and added them to stews, soups, and meats. Today, when planted, blueberry bushes produce fruit for 25 to 40 years. The peak harvest season is in July, which is also National Blueberry Month.

CANTALOUPE

Cantaloupe is a type of melon from the same gourd family as squashes and cucumbers and is planted each year.

MANGO

Mangoes originated in Southeast Asia and India and are grown in tropical and sub-tropical climates. Evergreen mango trees can grow up to 60 feet tall and produce fruit 4 to 6 years after planting.

PAPAYA

Papaya is a tropical fruit whose plants resemble trees but are technically large herbs. Papaya fruit is melon-like and can range from 6 to 20 inches long. The dried version is usually sweetened with fruit juice or sugar and sold in spears or diced.

PINEAPPLE

Pineapple fruits are produced by the flowers of the pineapple plant joining together to form a cone-shaped juicy fruit. Classified as an herb, pineapple plants are grown in the tropics, and fruit juice or sugar is typically added to the dried rings or chunks.

Health Benefits of Dried Fruits

Traditional dried fruits—apples, apricots, dates, figs, peaches, prunes, and raisins—provide a wealth of nutritional benefits and are considered side by side with recommendations for daily fruit intake. These dried fruits are nutrient dense and are naturally rich in vitamins, minerals, and phytochemicals, and provide an important source of fiber, potassium, and antioxidants.

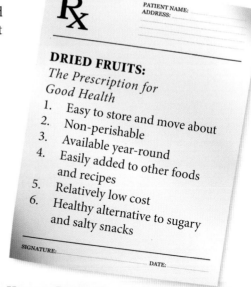

℞ PATIENT NAME:
ADDRESS:

DRIED FRUITS:
The Prescription for Good Health
1. Easy to store and move about
2. Non-perishable
3. Available year-round
4. Easily added to other foods and recipes
5. Relatively low cost
6. Healthy alternative to sugary and salty snacks

SIGNATURE: DATE:

FITNESS FUEL
Dried fruits can also help in maintaining a healthy weight, and are the perfect snack when on the go. Diets incorporating dried fruits have been linked with lower rates of obesity, lower diabetes, and lower rates of cancer.

	Valuable Nutrients	Health Benefits
RAISINS 	Contain **phytochemicals** and **boron**	Phytochemicals benefit oral health by fighting bacteria that cause cavities and gum disease. Boron is beneficial to bone health.
FIGS 	High source of **dietary fiber**	The fiber in figs is associated with improved digestive health and has been shown to have anti-clotting, antispasmodic, anti-ulcer, anti-cancer, and lipid-lowering properties.
APRICOTS 	Rich in carotenoids like **beta-carotene**	Beta-carotene is important for healthy eyes, skin, and a strong immune system.
PRUNES 	Rich in **phenolic compounds**	The phenolic compounds in prunes—neochlorogenic acid, chlorogenic acid, isoflavones, and lignans—promote bone health.
DATES 	High in **antioxidants** and **proanthocyanidins**	Antioxidants protect cells against free radicals, and proanthocyanidin compounds are strongly associated with cardiovascular health.
PEACHES 	Excellent source of **vitamin A**	Vitamin A is important for the retina and in maintaining healthy eyes.

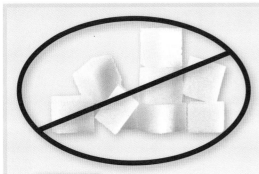

NO ADDED SUGAR
- Naturally sweet without the addition of sweeteners.
- Low glycemic index, possibly due to the presence of polyphenols, phenols, and tannins.

NATURAL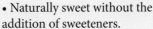
- Just *Fruit & Sunshine*®
- Dried fruit = fresh fruit with a reduced water content level.
- Raisins have nothing added, and many other dried fruits have added only a color preservative like sulfur dioxide.

| 19 |
| K |
| Potassium |
| 39.0983 |

5		12
B		Mg
Boron		Magnesium
10.811		24.3050

NUTRIENTS
- Significant source of potassium, which can help lower blood pressure.
- Provide calcium, magnesium, vitamin K, and boron—all beneficial to maintaining bone health.

HealthBenefits of Raisins & Dried Fruits

FAT FREE
- Naturally fat and cholesterol free.

NO ADDED SALT
- No added salt and low in sodium.

HIGH FIBER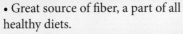
- Great source of fiber, a part of all healthy diets.
- High fiber diets are recommended to reduce the risk of cardiovascular disease, diabetes, and cancer.

SERVING SIZE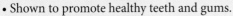
- A 1 ounce or 30 gram serving of raisins and other traditional dried fruits contains less than 100 calories.

DENTAL HEALTH
- Shown to promote healthy teeth and gums.
- Contain bioactive compounds with antimicrobial properties, capable of inhibiting the growth of bacteria that cause cavities and gum disease.

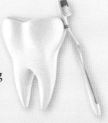

Healthy **100** Calories or less Per Ounce!

SUN·MAID
NATURAL CALIFORNIA
RAISINS

International Food Guidelines

Food guidelines around the world are educational tools used to help choose foods for well-balanced diets. While the guidelines take a variety of forms including pagodas, plates, spinning tops, pyramids, and wheels, there is one similarity between them all: fruits and vegetables are essential to good health. Some guidelines include recommendations for exercise and plenty of water, while others focus on food groups and proper portions. Grapes are pictured on many of the guidelines as illustrations and photographs, and a number feature images of dried fruit.

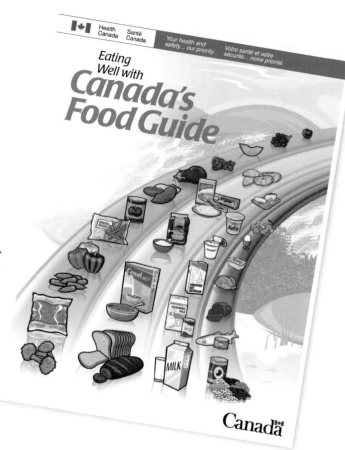

CANADA

With an image of grapes among its pictured fruits and vegetables, *Canada's Food Guide* lists foods in four groups. The guide, which was created to help reduce and prevent chronic disease, obesity, type 2 diabetes, and certain types of cancers, recommends eating a serving of fruits or vegetables at every meal.

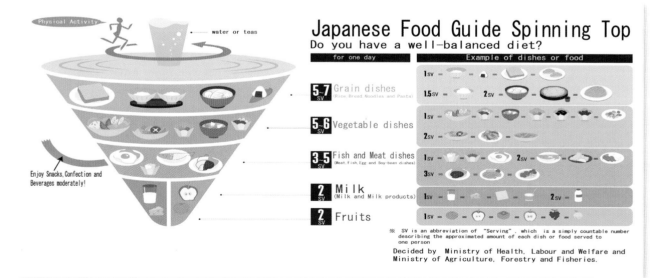

JAPAN

Japan's *Food Guide Spinning Top* uses plates of food both to show the recommended foods and to estimate the quantity of food that should be eaten. Included among the fruit group is an illustration of grapes.

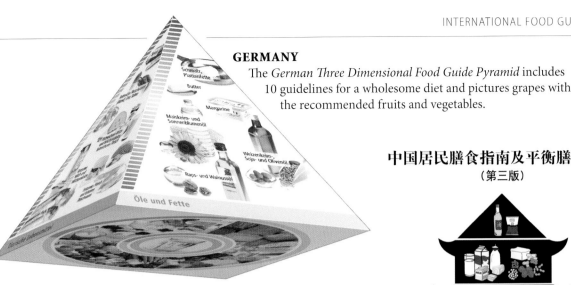

GERMANY

The *German Three Dimensional Food Guide Pyramid* includes 10 guidelines for a wholesome diet and pictures grapes with the recommended fruits and vegetables.

中国居民膳食指南及平衡膳食宝塔
（第三版）

油 25—30克
盐 6克

奶类及奶制品
200—400克
大豆类及坚果
30—50克

畜禽肉类
50—75克
鱼虾类
50—100克
蛋类
25—50克

蔬菜类
300—500克
水果类
200—400克

谷类薯类及杂豆
250—400克

水 1200毫升

CHINA

The *Balance Dietary Pagoda*, created by the Chinese Nutrition Society, includes an illustration of grapes in the second tier of the pagoda, and advises plenty of water and exercise.

식 품 구 성 탑

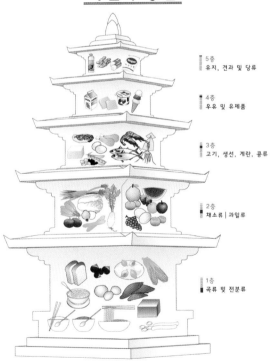

■ 5층
유지, 견과 및 당류

■ 4층
우유 및 유제품

■ 3층
고기, 생선, 계란, 콩류

■ 2층
채소류 | 과일류

■ 1층
곡류 및 전분류

INDIA

In addition to recommending that fruits and vegetables be eaten liberally, the *Dietary Guidelines for Indians* pyramid advises regular exercise and advises against drinking alcohol and smoking. Grapes are shown among the pictures of fruits and vegetables.

DIETARY GUIDELINES FOR INDIANS
Foundation to Nutrition and Health

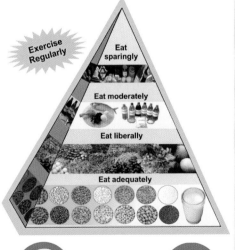

Exercise Regularly

Eat sparingly

Eat moderately

Eat liberally

Eat adequately

사단법인 **한국영양학회**

KOREA

Featuring grapes among its illustrated fruits, the Korean Nutrition Society created the *Food Guidance Pagoda* and recommends two servings of fruit daily for a 2,000 calorie diet.

International Food Guidelines

FOOD PYRAMID

For years, the food pyramid defined American guidelines for healthy eating. In 2005, the introduction of *MyPyramid* turned the original food pyramid, with its hierarchy of foods, on its side with each food group represented by a color. The pyramid also included a stick figure running up the side to show the need for exercise in addition to a healthy diet.

FROM PYRAMID TO PLATE

In 2011, the new food icon *MyPlate* again transformed the visual representation of a healthy diet in the United States, this time into a plate divided up into food groups of the same color as the previous version. While images of the foods themselves are not pictured, the icon is a visual representation of how to think about each meal, for example, that half the plate should be filled with fruits and vegetables.

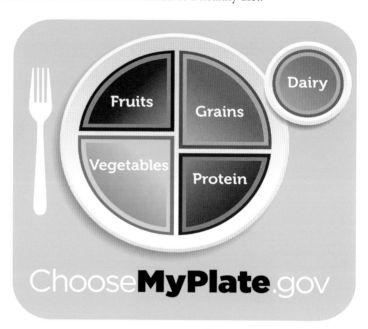

SWEDEN

Sweden's *Food Circle* was developed by the National Food Administration and pictures dried fruits in the group with other fruits.

DENMARK

Featuring an illustration of a carrot and apple to represent fruits and vegetables, Denmark's *Diet Compass* consists of eight groups including fruits and vegetables, maintaining a normal weight, and adequate amounts of fluids.

AUSTRALIA

The Australian Guide to Healthy Eating recommends 1 to 5 servings of fruit per day, depending on age and gender. The guide notes the importance of eating a variety of fruits including fresh, canned, and dried fruits.

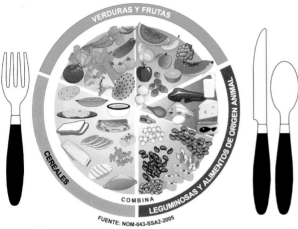

MEXICO

Featuring grapes among the colorful illustrations of fruits and vegetables, Mexico's *El Plato del Bien Comer*, or the Eat Well Plate, consists of three main groups: cereals; vegetables and fruits; and legumes and animal foods.

UNITED KINGDOM

With an image of dried fruit and grapes as examples of fruits and vegetables, the United Kingdom's *Eatwell Plate* is distributed by the Food Standards Agency, and recommends consuming 5 servings of fruits and vegetables daily.

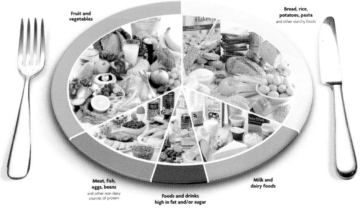

TURKEY

Turkey's food recommendations, entitled *Adequate and Balanced Nutrition,* identifies 50 nutrients that are necessary for proper growth and development, and displays four food groups in its guide, including illustrations of fruits and vegetables.

Raisins in Europe

With Greece, Spain, and other countries in the Mediterranean region supplying raisins and dried fruits to the rest of Europe for more than a thousand years, it was no wonder that cultures across the continent made raisins and dried fruits an integral part of their cuisines. At the turn of the 20th century, raisins from California were newcomers to the European market, and spotting an opportunity for expansion, Sun-Maid quickly embarked on a multinational and multilingual advertising campaign overseas.

RAISINS IN THE UNITED KINGDOM

Sun-Maid raisins were first introduced to the United Kingdom in 1916, and the October 1918 *Sun-Maid Herald* reported that consumption of raisins per capita in Great Britain was five times that of the United States. In 1922, Sun-Maid opened its London office. In the U.K., one of the most popular raisin dishes is fruitcake, which is made with mixed dried fruits, raisins, nuts and spices, and is commonly eaten during Christmas and at weddings.

U.S. BERLIN AIRLIFT

Americans to Fly Tons of Food Over Russian Blockade

Washington, D.C., July 1, 1948—The President announced U.S. efforts to airlift food to needy Germans due to the Russian

RAISIN RELIEF

In 1948, the Berlin Airlift brought supplies to the western section of Berlin blockaded by the Soviet Union. "Raisin Bomber" pilots collected raisins, candy, chocolate, and gum, and sewed them into miniature parachutes dropped to children waiting by the airfields below.

FINLAND

Sun-Maid tailors its advertising to individual markets, as this Finnish ad, circa 1924, demonstrates. The Finns use raisins in baking, in the cold drink *Sima*, and the hot drink *Glög*.

THE SWEDISH KITCHEN

Sun-Maid raisins are seen in this Swedish kitchen, where they are a part of many classic dishes. In Scandinavia, raisins are integral to holiday festivities. They are used in buns decorated with raisins to celebrate St. Lucia Day, in the Norwegian Christmas cake *Julekake*, and in *Vörtbröd*, a Swedish dark Christmas bread.

SUN-MAID IN DENMARK

Danes in traditional dress, with Sun-Maid packages in hand, flank a promotional window display for the *rosiner*, as raisins are known in Denmark. Some Danish Christmas traditions include decorating the tree with raisins. The Scandinavian country remains a solid market for these dried fruits, which are frequently used in baking.

HOLIDAY TRADITIONS

In ancient times, a typical breakfast for a wealthy Roman household included yeast breads with raisins, and through the centuries, raisin breads and cakes have taken many forms around the globe, often as a holiday treat. Fruitcakes combining dried fruits and nuts are a part of the Christmas tradition in many cultures. National specialties like German *stollen* and Dutch *skerstetol* can include almond paste in the middle of the loaf, while regional variations produce the light Milanese *panettone* and the dense Tuscan *panforte*. The Spanish *roscón de reyes* is baked in a wreath shape, while the Czech *vánočka* is braided. Poland's *makowiec* is a poppy seed cake topped with raisins, and Austria's *gugelhupf* is a light-colored bundt cake.

United Kingdom—fruitcake

Germany—stollen

Portugal—bolo rei

Czech Republic—vánočka

Poland—makowiec

Austria—gugelhupf

RAISINS IN GERMANY

German cuisine incorporates raisins and dried fruits into both sweet and savory dishes, such as classic breads and stews. *Sauerbraten* is a beef stew flavored with red wine and raisins. It is traditionally served with red cabbage, potatoes, potato dumplings, *spätzle*, or noodles.

IRISH SODA BREAD

Raisins and caraway seeds are combined into a buttermilk dough to make Irish soda bread. Some recipes call for soaking the raisins ahead of time in whiskey.

RUGELACH

A traditional Jewish pastry, *rugelach* means "little twist" in Yiddish. To prepare, dough is filled with raisins, nuts, and/or fruit preserves, then rolled into a crescent shape similar to a croissant.

Raisins in Asia

Sun-Maid began developing raisin markets in Asia in 1918, and by 1922 had set up offices in Japan and China. In China, raisins were marketed as a wholesome breakfast food—raisin bread and rice flavored with California raisins became popular dishes. Demand for California raisins quickly grew in Japan, where they were readily incorporated into raisin bread and raisin cakes. Today, 70 percent of all raisins consumed in Japan are in baked goods. Trade expanded into the Philippines, Malaysia, and Indonesia, where each country has found unique ways of adding California raisins into their cuisines.

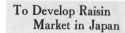

To Develop Raisin Market in Japan

Nippon Raisin Kaisha is the name of a Tokyo company incorporated recently to handle raisins exclusively. C. A. Paulden, of our Advertising and Sales Department, who is making a tour of the Orient in an effort to broaden existing raisin markets and to create new ones, has written a letter to the Associated, dated Yokohama, in which he states he has given the Japanese raisin agency to Shimizu Bros. of Yokohama.

These brothers have associated with them in a recently incorporated company Y. Nakamoto, who, by the way, is the father of K. Nakamoto, of the Contract Department of the Associated in Fresno. One of the brothers is a large wholesale grocer, and the other has a large wholesale bakery establishment. The new firm will have its main office at Tokyo, with branches at Yokohama and Osaka.

INDIA

In India, *biryani*—a rice-based entrée—appears in dozens of regional variations featuring meats, fish, eggs, or vegetables. Raisins are often combined with yogurt and other fruits on the list of ingredients. Another Indian dish, *kheer*, is a sweet pudding made from rice and milk flavored with cardamom, raisins, and nuts, which is enjoyed during feasts and celebrations, including *Diwali*, the festival of lights.

This raisin box from 1922 (*right*) markets Sun-Maid raisins to China, where they are incorporated into traditional dishes. Sun-Maid raisins are shipped to China in large boxes. This 1927 photograph (*far right*) shows the raisins being repacked into smaller containers to be sold in grocery stores and markets. Chinese raisin dishes include *sacima*—a snack made of fried noodles in syrup with dried fruits and nuts—and *shouzhuafan* (also known as *zinjiang* rice), which is rice cooked with lamb, carrots, onion, and dried fruits, such as raisins, apricots, or dates.

TAIWAN

A Sun-Maid box adorns the side of a delivery truck in Taiwan, one of the 50 countries where Sun-Maid sells its products. Other key markets in Asia include Japan, China, Korea, the Philippines, Singapore, Malaysia, Indonesia, Hong Kong, India, New Zealand, Vietnam, and Cambodia.

MALAYSIA

Kindergarten students in Malaysia participate in an educational program featuring Sun-Maid's Mini-Snacks. In addition to sponsoring school programs, Sun-Maid also promotes cooking classes featuring raisins. Malaysian raisin specialties include rice dishes such as *biryani* and *minyak* rice, along with pineapple fried rice.

PHILIPPINES

In the Philippines, raisin recipes include bread pudding called *budin*, the pork and potato stew *menudo*, and the rolled meatloaf *embutido*.

JAPAN

Raisin breads, cakes, and pastries are popular bakery choices to Japanese consumers, where most raisins are used in the form of baked goods. Sun-Maid works with partners such as the Culinary Institute of America to develop new raisin recipes and promote ongoing innovation in the field of baking.

INDONESIA

At right, an Indonesian grocery store shelf is stocked with Sun-Maid raisins. Above, a chef instructor adds raisins to complete a dish during a Sun-Maid-sponsored cooking seminar in Indonesia. Indonesian cuisine varies across the 6,000 populated islands that make up the nation and combines influences from India, the Middle East, China, and Europe. Raisins can be used in the Indonesian recipes for *Javanese cassava cake* and *rice kebuli*—rice cooked with raisins, nuts, cinnamon, and lamb.

Raisin Bread

For as long as people have been baking bread, bakers have made raisin bread. Raisin breads take many forms around the globe. In the early 1900s, Sun-Maid used raisin bread to introduce California raisins, providing both ingredients and recipes to bakers across the country, who in turn baked loaves of raisin bread by the millions. Today, Sun-Maid Raisin Bread is widely distributed throughout the United States and Canada.

ADVERTISING THE BEST

This 1916 ad labeled raisins and raisin bread "The True Fruit-Food." Large train shipments of raisins made the key raisin bread ingredient available to customers in the East, and the popularity of new recipes increased demand.

PRIZE-WINNING RAISINS

Sun-Maid raisins won the first place prize for seeded raisins at the 1915 Panama Pacific International Exposition held in San Francisco. At the fair, raisin ambassadors known as "sun maids" passed out raisin boxes, raisin recipes, and raisin bread to fair visitors, many who were sampling raisins for the first time. In April 1915, a raisin bread-baking contest was held, and following the fair, Sun-Maid made its raisin bread recipe available to bakers so consumers across the country could enjoy "California's raisin bread made with Sun-Maid raisins."

AT THE BAKERY

A Sun-Maid display is shown in this 1926 photograph of a typical bakery of its time. Raisin bread was advertised as being more filling and nutritious than plain breads, since the addition of raisins provided much-needed nutrients including iron and potassium. In order to sell loaves labeled "raisin bread" in the U.S., the government standard requires that every 100 pounds of flour is matched by 50 pounds of raisins.

MORE RAISINS!!

Sun-Maid Raisin Bread was introduced as a licensed product in 1980. With 50 percent more raisins than required standards, a cinnamon swirl, strong Sun-Maid brand image, and red package, the bread quickly became a top seller in the raisin bread category.

JAPANESE RAISIN BREADS

Raisin rolls are baked in a factory in Japan, where the majority of raisins are used in baked goods, such as breads, rolls, and cakes. The California raisin industry has promoted the development of Japanese raisin bread recipes since 1949 by sponsoring annual baking classes and seminars focusing specifically on raisin breads.

MAKING PANETTONE

Legend has it that *panettone* was first created when a baker named Toni accidentally spilled raisins and crystallized fruit into a batch of bread. While other stories dispute how and when panettone was first invented, the Christmas bread holds a special place in the hearts of many cultures around the world. Panettone bakers consider the complex process of making the bread a labor of love, a labor whose success depends entirely on the bread's yeast.

1. Water and flour are added to the mother yeast.

2. Vegetable shortening, sugar, eggs, and more flour and water are added before being mixed in an industrial mixer.

3. After the dough is allowed to rise for several hours, it is beaten again and the raisins, dried fruits, or chocolate pieces are added.

4. The dough rises again after being placed in paper molds, and is then transported into the oven by conveyor belts.

Founded in 1952, the Brazilian company *Bauducco* bakes panettone using Sun-Maid raisins, with the bread available only during the Christmas season.

The Future

The past 100 years have seen California farming transformed, with the horse-drawn plow replaced by precision farming using global positioning systems. Sun-Maid farmers have seen dramatic changes in the world around them, too. A century ago, man was making his first awkward flights in single engine bi-planes, but today, passenger flights are commonplace. In 1915, the first U.S. coast-to-coast telephone call was made from New York to San Francisco, but now almost everyone has a cell phone.

Mobile electronic devices link consumers, families, and businesses with instant information in the form of streaming visuals, music, and text—all of which is available 24 hours a day, from any location, and in virtually every language. Today, all it takes is the touch of a screen to find information on any product, its use, or to purchase goods shipped from anywhere in the world. Furthermore, recipe books are being replaced with electronic books and mobile access.

A CENTURY OF PROGRESS
Right: Sun-Maid raisins are hauled to the packing house in 1915.
Below: an airplane painted with the words "Sun-Maid, S.E. Brush, Pilot" in 1920. *Below right*: a modern commercial jet enables easier worldwide travel and commerce.

EVOLVING COMMUNICATIONS
The telephone is among the many technologies that has advanced during Sun-Maid's century of experience, from the earliest models to the first mobile phones and beyond.

GOING MOBILE

QR codes—short for Quick Response codes—printed on Sun-Maid packages send consumers to mobile-optimized web pages and interactive content. Other mobile applications, including Recipe.com and downloadable recipe books enable instant access to raisin and dried fruit information and recipes.

The future holds tremendous opportunity for raisins and dried fruits, which grow best in a limited number of unique climates and easily travel the globe to satisfy customers. Instead of circulating recipe books and printed information, the mobile information age will allow Sun-Maid to link customers around the world with "everything they want to know" on growing practices, sustainability, product specifications, nutritional information, and the most enticing raisin and dried fruit recipes for every culture and celebration.

Information technology and international commerce will continue to further close the distance between the grapevine and the consumer. Sun-Maid's vision is to successfully build on our legacy and use the best available technologies to "serve American families and the world for the next 100 years."

CHAPTER 6
Recipes

Prize Raisin Bread

From 1915 Sun-Maid recipe book.

Featured in the **Souvenir California Raisin Recipe Book** created for the 1915 Panama Pacific International Exposition, this Prize Raisin Bread recipe was selected from thousands submitted.

Makes: 3 loaves

INGREDIENTS

1 (¼-ounce) package active dry yeast
1½ cups potato water*
About 9½ cups all-purpose flour, divided
2 cups milk
3 tablespoons granulated sugar
1 tablespoon lard or butter
1 tablespoon salt
1 (15-ounce) package Sun-Maid Natural Raisins

METHOD

1. Stir yeast into potato water in a large mixing bowl. Let stand 10 minutes to dissolve.
2. Mix in 3 cups flour, stirring well with a wooden spoon (or mix with paddle attachment of an electric mixer). Cover and let stand at room temperature overnight, or until risen.
3. Heat milk in a saucepan or microwaveable container, just until little bubbles break the surface; add sugar, lard or butter, and salt. Cool to lukewarm.
4. Mix milk with the yeast mixture. Gradually stir or beat in 6 cups flour to make a stiff dough, about 10 minutes.
5. Add raisins; knead on a lightly floured surface until dough is smooth and elastic. Place in a large, lightly oiled bowl. Cover and let rise at room temperature until doubled, about 1½ hours.
6. Preheat oven to 350°F.
7. Shape into 3 loaves. Place in greased 9 x 5-inch loaf pans.
8. Bake 1 hour or until golden brown and bread sounds hollow when tapped. Cool in pans 15 minutes; remove to a wire rack to cool completely.
9. For a softer crust, brush tops with water and sprinkle lightly with granulated sugar.

*Water used for boiling potatoes, cooled to lukewarm.

Japanese Rice Flour Raisin Bread

Makes: 3 loaves

INGREDIENTS
3³/₄ cups warm water
1 teaspoon active dry yeast
2 teaspoons agave syrup (or
    1 tablespoon granulated sugar)
3³/₄ cup rice flour
1 tablespoon softened butter
2 teaspoons salt
5 to 6 cups bread flour
3 cups raisins
3 cups dried apples
1 cup chopped peanuts

Recipe courtesy of **RAC Japan**.

METHOD

1. In a large bowl, combine water, yeast, agave syrup, and stir to dissolve. Set aside at room temperature until foamy, about 10 minutes.

2. Stir in rice flour, butter, salt, and enough bread flour to create a firm dough. Turn out onto a floured surface and knead 8 to 10 minutes, until smooth and elastic. Add more flour only as needed to reduce stickiness. Return to the mixing bowl, dust the top lightly with flour, and cover with a damp cloth or plastic wrap. Rise at room temperature until doubled in volume, about 1 hour. Punch dough down and let rise again until doubled, another 30 minutes.

3. Coat three 9 x 5-inch loaf pans with pan spray, and line the bottom and short sides with a strip of parchment paper. Turn risen dough out onto floured surface, and with a rolling pin, roll into an 18 x 24-inch rectangle. Mix together raisins, apples, and peanuts and sprinkle evenly across the dough. Starting on a long edge, roll the dough up into a log. Cut the log into three 8-inch loaves, and place into pan seam-side down. Dust with flour, cover with plastic wrap, and rise again for 30 minutes. Preheat oven to 350°F.

4. Bake until golden brown and hollow sounding, about 40 to 60 minutes. The internal temperature should reach 210°F. Cool for 10 minutes, remove loaf from the pan, and cool completely on a rack.

Corn Flour Raisin Cake

Makes: about 20 pieces

INGREDIENTS
¹/₂ cup Sun-Maid raisins
1³/₄ cups all-purpose flour
1 cup finely ground cornmeal
1 teaspoon active dry yeast

Recipe courtesy of **Betty's Kitchen Magazine**.

METHOD

1. Rinse and drain raisins to moisten. Set aside.

2. Mix flour, cornmeal, and yeast in a large bowl. Add enough water to form a soft dough.

3. Lightly coat a baking pan (9 x 9 or 9 x 13-inch) with oil and sprinkle with half the raisins. Place dough in pan. Let rise until double, about 1 hour.

4. Top with remaining raisins. Bake in steam oven for 35 to 40 minutes until set. Cut into squares to serve.

Almond Laced Saffron Naan with Raisins

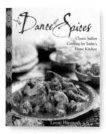

From **The Dance of Spices: Classic Indian Cooking for Today's Home Kitchen**; Wiley 2005; reprinted with permission from the publisher, and author Laxmi Hiremath.

The oven-baked flatbread naan has many variations, including those livened up with golden raisins and spices.

Makes: 12 naans

INGREDIENTS

4 cups unbleached all-purpose flour plus additional for dusting
2 teaspoons baking powder
1 teaspoon sugar
1 teaspoon salt
1 teaspoon active dry yeast
$^{1}/_{2}$ cup plain yogurt
1 large egg, slightly beaten
3 tablespoons oil
1 teaspoon saffron threads dissolved in 2 tablespoons hot milk
$^{1}/_{2}$ cup warm, whole, or 2% low-fat milk
$^{1}/_{4}$ cup plus 2 tablespoons warm water
Thinly sliced almonds
$^{1}/_{2}$ cup raisins
Cornmeal for the peel or baking sheet

METHOD

1. Combine the flour, baking powder, sugar, salt, and yeast in a food processor, and pulse until mixed. Add the yogurt, egg, oil, and saffron mixture. Pulse until crumbly. With the machine running, gradually add milk, then the water through the feed tube in a steady stream. Process until the dough comes together into a ball and begins to clean the sides of the bowl.

2. Place dough on a work surface; lightly coat both your hands with oil and knead well for 6 to 8 minutes, the dough should be medium-soft, and hold an impression when pressed. Form into a smooth ball, cover loosely with kitchen towel and let rest in a draft-free spot for 4 to 6 hours or until the dough doubles in volume.

3. Lightly oil your hands, punch down the dough, and place on a floured work surface and knead briefly until smooth. Divide into 12 portions, and roll each portion between your hands to form a smooth ball, put on a baking sheet about 2 inches apart and cover with a kitchen towel; set aside until the dough doubles in volume, for 15 minutes. Place a ball of dough on lightly floured work surface and roll it out into a 5-inch circle or oval shape and a tad more than ⅛-inch thick, dusting lightly with flour as necessary. Sprinkle some almonds and raisins; press firmly and finish the naan.

4. Repeat with remaining dough. Brush the tops of each naan with water, oil, or butter. Preheat the oven to 500°F. Sprinkle cornmeal on a baker's peel or the backside of a large baking sheet. Place 2 to 3 naans on prepared baker's peel or sheet, brush the tops with water, slide naans directly onto the pizza stone or quarry tiles (do not use a baking sheet). Bake 4 or 5 minutes until lightly speckled. Transfer in a cloth-lined basket. Naans are at their best when hot.

Saint Lucia Buns

In Sweden, the day of Saint Lucia is celebrated on December 13 with lightly sweetened saffron buns decorated with raisins.

Makes: 20 buns

INGREDIENTS

1 cup butter, melted
$^1/_2$ teaspoon saffron threads, finely crumbled
1 cup milk
$^3/_4$ cup granulated sugar
1 teaspoon salt
2 packages ($^1/_4$-ounce each) active dry yeast
6 cups all-purpose flour
2 eggs
$^1/_2$ cup Sun-Maid Natural Raisins or currants, plus more for decorating
1 egg white

METHOD

1. Crumble saffron threads into melted butter. Let stand 30 minutes for flavor to intensify.

2. Heat milk just to a simmer then immediately remove from heat. Stir in melted butter, sugar, and salt. Pour into mixing bowl and cool until just warm to the touch. Stir in yeast and let stand 10 minutes.

3. Beat $3^1/_2$ cups flour into yeast mixture. Stir in eggs until well blended. Add just enough of the remaining flour to form a soft dough and it pulls away from the sides of the bowl. Dough should be very soft but not too sticky.

4. Transfer dough to a large greased bowl and turn to coat all sides. Cover with a clean towel and let rise until doubled, about 1 hour.

5. Punch down dough. Knead lightly two or three times on a floured surface. Pinch off golf ball size pieces and roll into $^1/_2$-inch thick ropes. Shape into S-shapes, coiling the ends. Place on a baking sheet. Cover with a towel and let rise until doubled, about 30 minutes.

6. Preheat oven to 375°F.

7. Brush buns with egg white and place one raisin in the center of each coiled end.

8. Bake until golden brown, 15 to 18 minutes. Wrap airtight to store.

Stollen

Recipe courtesy of the **King Arthur Flour Company**, kingarthurflour.com

Stollen is a fruitcake made with raisins, mixed dried fruits, nuts, and spices baked into a loaf shape and covered with powdered sugar. Some stollens include a ribbon of marzipan and the traditional weight of a stollen is about 4.4 pounds, or 2 kilograms. During the Christmas season, the cake is called a *Christstollen*. Dresden, Germany celebrates an annual Stollenfest each December to honor the traditional cake.

Makes: 2 stollen, about 14 servings each

INGREDIENTS

SPONGE
1 cup King Arthur Unbleached All-Purpose Flour
½ cup water
2 teaspoons instant yeast

DOUGH
2½ cups King Arthur Unbleached All-Purpose Flour
¼ cup (½ stick) butter, cut into small cubes
1 egg
¼ cup milk
⅓ cup sugar
1¼ teaspoons salt
4 teaspoons instant yeast
1 teaspoon almond extract
1 teaspoon vanilla extract
½ cup chopped dates
½ cup golden raisins
½ cup candied cherries, coarsely chopped*
2 tablespoons King Arthur Unbleached All-Purpose Flour
½ cup slivered almonds, toasted

TOPPING
1½ tablespoons butter, melted
Confectioners' sugar

*The easiest way to chop candied cherries, which tend to be very sticky, is by snipping each in half with a pair of scissors.

Note: For a more traditional stollen, substitute ½ cup candied peel, citron, or angelica for the ½ cup chopped dates.

METHOD

SPONGE
1. Combine the flour, water, and yeast in a large mixing bowl, stirring till smooth. (Or use your bread machine, canceling the machine after several minutes of mixing.)

2. Let the mixture rest overnight at room temperature.

DOUGH
1. Add the flour, butter, egg, milk, sugar, salt, yeast, almond extract, and vanilla to the sponge. Stir to combine, then knead thoroughly, using your hands, an electric mixer, a food processor, or a bread machine, till the dough is very smooth and supple.

2. Transfer the dough to a lightly greased bowl (or leave it in the bread machine), cover the bowl, and allow the dough to rise for 1 to 1½ hours. It probably won't double in bulk, but will become puffy.

3. While the dough is rising, stir together the dates, raisins, cherries, flour, and almonds. Transfer the dough to a clean, lightly greased work surface. Knead the fruit into the dough until it is well-distributed; a good way to do this is to pat or roll the dough into a rough 12 x 15-inch rectangle, press the fruit and nuts evenly over its surface, then roll it up like a jelly roll, starting with a long edge. Divide the roll into two pieces, shape each piece into a rough 9-inch log, cover the logs, and let them rest for 10 minutes.

4. Pat each log into a 10 x 8-inch oval. The fruit may try to "fall out" of the dough; that's OK, just stick it back in. Fold each oval lengthwise, bringing one side over the other but leaving a 1-inch gap, as if you were making a Parker House roll (in other words, fold the dough not quite in half). Press the edge of the top half to seal it to the bottom half, tent the dough with lightly greased plastic wrap, and allow it to rise for 2 hours, or until it's noticeably puffy.

5. Bake the stollen in a preheated 350°F oven for 30 to 35 minutes, tenting it with aluminum foil after 20 minutes if it appears to be browning too quickly. The finished loaves should be golden brown, and their internal temperature should register 190°F on an instant-read thermometer.

6. Remove the stollen from the oven, and brush them with melted butter. Transfer them to a rack to cool completely. When the stollen are cool, dust them heavily with confectioners' sugar.

Royal Wedding Cake

Traditional wedding cake in the United Kingdom is a dense, not-too-sweet fruitcake, unlike the dark fruitcakes typically served at Christmas. Our adapted version is filled with apricots, cherries, golden raisins, and green pistachios for a colorful contrast. Lots of orange and lemon zest add a tangy touch.

Makes: one 7 or 8-inch cake

INGREDIENTS

10 tablespoons butter, softened
¾ cup granulated sugar, preferably superfine baker's sugar
2 eggs
1½ cups all-purpose flour
¾ cup Sun-Maid Tart Cherries
¾ cup Sun-Maid Dried Apricots, coarsely chopped
⅔ cup Sun-Maid Golden Raisins
½ cup shelled pistachios, whole or broken
⅓ cup chopped candied citrus peel
¼ cup chopped candied ginger
Zest of one orange
Zest of one lemon
3 tablespoons orange juice
1 tablespoon lemon juice
Purchased white fondant, optional

METHOD

1. Preheat oven to 325°F. Line the bottom of a 7 or 8-inch springform pan with parchment paper for easier removal. Coat paper and sides of pan with cooking spray.

2. Beat butter and sugar with an electric mixer until creamy. Beat in eggs.

3. Add flour and mix well.

4. Stir in dried fruit, citrus peel, and ginger. Mix well.

5. Add zest and juices. Stir just to combine. Pour into prepared pan and smooth top.

6. Bake 45 minutes; reduce temperature to 300°F and continue baking for an additional 1 hour and 15 to 30 minutes or until golden brown and dry crumbs cling to a pick inserted in center. Top will be slightly cracked. Cool in pan 15 minutes. Remove sides and cool completely.

7. Wrap well and refrigerate for up to 1 month. Traditionally, this cake may be drizzled periodically with alcohol of choice or fruit juice during the month.

8. Cover with rolled fondant before serving, if desired.

Hot Cross Buns

From 1964 Sun-Maid
recipe book.

Makes: 24 rolls

INGREDIENTS

$^1/_2$ **cup warm water (110 to 115°F)**
2 packages ($^1/_4$ ounce) active dry yeast
$^3/_4$ **cup milk**
$^1/_2$ **cup butter**
$^1/_2$ **cup granulated sugar**
$^1/_2$ **teaspoon salt**
1 large egg
4 cups all-purpose flour or 2 cups each
all-purpose flour and whole
wheat flour
1 teaspoon cinnamon
$^1/_4$ **teaspoon nutmeg**
1 cup Sun-Maid Natural Raisins
1 egg yolk

GLAZE
1 cup powdered sugar
1 tablespoon milk
$^1/_2$ **teaspoon vanilla extract**

METHOD

1. Stir warm water and yeast in a large mixing bowl or stand mixer bowl.
2. Heat milk and butter in a saucepan or microwave until 120°F, or very warm, but not hot to the touch. Butter does not need to completely melt.
3. Stir in sugar and salt.
4. Add milk mixture, egg, 2 cups flour, cinnamon, and nutmeg to yeast. Beat until smooth.
5. Gradually mix in remaining flour. Stir in raisins. Dough will be soft and slightly sticky.
6. Cover and let rise in draft-free place for 1 hour until about doubled in bulk or, cover and refrigerate several hours or up to overnight.
7. Punch down dough and divide into 24 equal pieces. Roll into balls and place on greased or parchment-lined baking sheet.
8. Mix egg yolk with 2 teaspoons water; brush on tops of dough balls. Let rise 30 minutes.
9. Bake in preheated 375°F oven for 25 to 30 minutes until golden brown. Cool on a wire rack.
10. Stir glaze ingredients to make a smooth frosting-like consistency. Scoop into a zip-top plastic sandwich bag and snip one corner. Squeeze in a cross over cooled rolls.

VARIATION: Add ½ cup mixed chopped candied fruits with raisins or 1 tablespoon grated orange zest to milk mixture.

Sunny Whole Wheat Currant Scones

Talk about a power breakfast. These scones are a high source of manganese, an antioxidant that also helps produce insulin, and folate, a B vitamin that helps fight anemia. Their hearty texture is great with a cup of tea.

From 2007 Sun-Maid Recipe Book **Fruit & Sunshine**.

Makes: 1 dozen scones

INGREDIENTS

1 cup white whole-wheat flour
1 cup whole-wheat flour
2 teaspoons baking powder
$\frac{1}{2}$ teaspoon baking soda
$\frac{1}{2}$ teaspoon ground nutmeg
$\frac{1}{2}$ teaspoon salt
6 tablespoons cold butter, cut up
1 cup Sun-Maid Natural Zante Currants
$\frac{1}{2}$ cup coarsely chopped walnuts, optional
2 tablespoons plus 2 teaspoons granulated sugar, divided
$\frac{3}{4}$ cup low-fat buttermilk
2 teaspoons egg white

METHOD

1. Heat oven to 375°F.
2. Combine flours, baking powder, baking soda, nutmeg, and salt in large bowl. Cut in butter until mixture is the texture of coarse bread crumbs.
3. Add currants, walnuts, and 2 tablespoons sugar and toss to mix evenly.
4. Stir in buttermilk with a fork until a soft dough forms.
5. Shape dough into a ball on a lightly floured surface. Divide into 2 parts and shape into 2 round balls.
6. Press into 6-inch rounds and place on an ungreased cookie sheet. Cut each round into 6 wedges, but do not separate the wedges. Brush with beaten egg white and sprinkle with 2 teaspoons sugar.
7. Bake for 20 to 22 minutes until golden brown. Break into wedges and serve warm.

TIP: If necessary, add 1 to 2 tablespoons water to moisten all of the flour.

Cinnamon-Raisin Biscuits

Makes: about 12 biscuits
Preparation time: 10 minutes
Total time: 25 minutes

INGREDIENTS

$1\frac{3}{4}$ cups all-purpose flour
$2\frac{1}{2}$ teaspoons baking powder
$\frac{1}{2}$ teaspoon salt
2 tablespoons sugar
1 teaspoon ground cinnamon
$\frac{1}{3}$ cup raisins and/or cherries
About $1\frac{1}{4}$ cups whipping (heavy) cream

From **Betty Crocker Christmas Cookbook**; Wiley 2010; reprinted with permission from the publisher.

METHOD

1. Heat oven to 450°F. In large bowl, mix flour, baking powder, and salt. Then add sugar, cinnamon, and raisins and/or cherries. Stir in just enough whipping cream so dough leaves side of bowl and forms a ball. (If dough is too dry, mix in 1 to 2 teaspoons more whipping cream.)
2. Place dough on lightly floured surface; gently roll in flour to coat. Knead lightly 10 times, sprinkling with flour if dough is too sticky. Roll or pat ½-inch thick. Cut with floured 2-inch biscuit cutter. On ungreased cookie sheet, place biscuits about 1 inch apart.
3. Bake 10 to 12 minutes or until golden brown. Immediately remove from cookie sheet to wire rack. Serve hot.

Plum Good Breakfast Oatmeal

Prunes, apple, and cinnamon dress up old-fashioned oatmeal. Adding an egg makes for an extra nutritious breakfast.

Makes: 2 to 3 servings

INGREDIENTS
1 cup apple juice
$^1/_2$ cup water
$^2/_3$ cup old-fashioned or quick oats
$^1/_2$ cup Sun-Maid Pitted Prunes, chopped
$^1/_2$ cup chopped apple
2 tablespoons chopped walnuts or pecans
$^1/_4$ teaspoon cinnamon
$^1/_8$ teaspoon salt (optional)
$^1/_3$ cup milk
1 egg

From 2009 Sun-Maid recipe book **Breakfast & Brunch**.

METHOD
1. Combine juice, water, oats, prunes, apple, nuts, cinnamon, and salt in medium saucepan. Bring to a boil over high heat.
2. Reduce heat and simmer uncovered; stirring occasionally until thickened and water is absorbed, 3 to 5 minutes for old-fashioned oats, 2 to 3 minutes for quick oats.
3. Whisk together milk and egg. Stir into hot cereal; simmer and stir for 1 minute.
4. Serve immediately with brown sugar and milk or cream, if desired.

Granola

Ladies' HomeJournal

Originally published in the October 2008 issue of **Ladies' Home Journal®** **Magazine**. ©2008 Meredith Corporation. All rights reserved.

Makes: 14 cups
Prep time: 10 minutes plus cooling
Baking time: 20 to 25 minutes

INGREDIENTS
2 cups packed brown sugar
$^2/_3$ cup butter or margarine
$^1/_2$ cup honey
4 cups uncooked oats
2 cups crisp rice cereal
2 tablespoons ground cinnamon
2 cups sliced blanched almonds
2 cups raisins
1 cup dried apples, diced
Milk, vanilla soy milk, or frozen yogurt (optional)

METHOD
1. Arrange oven racks in center and upper third of oven. Heat oven to 350°F. Line 2 jelly-roll pans with foil.
2. Heat sugar, butter, and honey in a medium saucepan over medium-high heat about 5 minutes, until butter is melted and sugar is dissolved.
3. Meanwhile, combine oats, rice cereal, cinnamon, and almonds in a large bowl.
4. Pour melted-butter mixture over oat mixture and toss to coat. Divide and spread mixture between prepared pans. Bake 20 to 25 minutes, stirring every 10 minutes, rotating sheets between racks until granola is toasted.
5. Cool granola on pans, 5 minutes, then transfer to a large bowl. Stir in raisins and apples and cool completely.

Banana French Toast

Makes: 4 servings

INGREDIENTS

8 slices Sun-Maid Raisin Bread
2 medium bananas cut in ¼-inch
slices
1 cup milk
4 ounces softened cream cheese
3 eggs
⅓ cup sugar
3 tablespoons all-purpose flour
2 teaspoons vanilla extract
Powdered sugar (optional)

METHOD

1. Heat oven to 350°F.

2. Place four slices of raisin bread in a single layer in a buttered 9-inch square baking dish. Top with bananas and four slices of raisin bread.

3. Blend milk, cream cheese, eggs, sugar, flour, and vanilla in a blender or food processor until smooth.

4. Pour over raisin bread. Let stand 5 minutes or refrigerate overnight.

5. Bake 40 to 45 minutes (50 to 55 minutes if refrigerated) until set and top is toasted. Let stand 10 minutes.

6. Cut French toast into diagonal halves and remove with spatula. Dust servings with powdered sugar if desired.

Sun-Maid's first French toast recipe appeared in the 1926 book **Recipes with Raisins**.

Baked Apples with Granola

From **Pillsbury Fast & Healthy Meals for Kids**; Wiley 2010; reprinted with permission from the publisher.

Makes: 2 servings
Preparation time:
10 minutes
Total time: 15 minutes

INGREDIENTS

1 large crisp apple (such as Braeburn, Gala, or Fuji)
1 tablespoon raisins or sweetened dried cranberries
1 tablespoon packed brown sugar
2 teaspoons margarine or butter, softened
$\frac{1}{2}$ cup low-fat fruit granola

METHOD

1. Cut apple in half lengthwise. With spoon, remove and discard core, making at least a 1-inch indentation in each apple half. Place each half in small microwaveable bowl.

2. Fill each apple half evenly with raisins and brown sugar; dot with margarine. Cover each with microwaveable plastic wrap, venting one corner.

3. Microwave each apple half on high 2 minutes 30 seconds to 3 minutes or until apple is tender. Top each with granola. If desired, serve with a little milk, cream, or fruit-flavored yogurt.

TIPS: What an ideal dessert treat for kids to make themselves. You can teach them how to cover with plastic wrap for microwaving. Let them sprinkle on their own granola at the end.

GOOD EATS FOR KIDS: Apples are a good source of vitamins A and C, and taste great, too.

Make-Your-Own Muesli

Muesli is an oats or flaked grain-based cereal chock full of dried fruits and nuts. Some recipes call for toasting the grains, but traditional Swiss recipes usually do not. It can be served raw, or soaked overnight in enough milk, yogurt, or fruit juice to moisten. Serve topped with fresh fruit if desired.

Makes: about 10 servings, ¹/₂ cup each

INGREDIENTS

4 cups oats or combination oats,
  rye, and wheat flakes
¹/₂ **cup Sun-Maid Raisins**
¹/₂ **cup Sun-Maid Apricots, chopped**
¹/₂ **cup chopped nuts**
¹/₄ **cup flaked coconut**

METHOD

1. Combine all ingredients and store in an airtight container.

SERVING VARIATIONS:

1. This is an approximate ratio of ingredients. Experiment with different amounts and varieties of dried fruit to make your own favorite cereal.

2. Cold Muesli—Combine ¹/₄ cup cereal with ¹/₂ cup yogurt, milk, or fruit juice; soak for 5 to 10 minutes or overnight.

3. Hot Muesli—Mix ¹/₂ cup muesli with ¹/₂ cup milk or water in a saucepan or microwaveable bowl. Bring just to a boil, simmer 3 to 5 minutes.

4. Add chopped apple, peaches, nectarines, or berries during soaking or cooking, if desired.

Sun-Maid's 1916 recipe book included instructions for using raisins and chopped dates to make breakfast cereals.

Date Shakes

Low-Fat Date Yogurt Shake

Makes: 1 serving

INGREDIENTS
¹/₂ **cup chopped California dates**
¹/₂ **medium banana**
¹/₂ **cup orange juice**
¹/₂ **cup plain nonfat yogurt**
¹/₂ **cup crushed ice**

METHOD
1. Combine first three ingredients in blender and puree until dates are finely chopped. Add yogurt and ice; blend until just combined.

Tropical Date Shake

Makes: 1 serving

INGREDIENTS
¹/₂ **cup California dates**
¹/₂ **cup pineapple juice**
2 **tablespoons shredded coconut**
1¹/₂ **teaspoons light rum, (optional)**
3 **scoops vanilla frozen yogurt**

METHOD
1. Combine all ingredients except frozen yogurt in blender and puree until dates are finely chopped.
2. Add frozen yogurt; blend until just combined.

Orange Date Shake

Makes: 1 serving

INGREDIENTS
¹/₂ **cup California dates**
¹/₂ **cup orange juice**
3 **scoops vanilla frozen yogurt**

METHOD
1. Combine dates and orange juice in blender and puree until dates are finely chopped.
2. Add frozen yogurt; blend until just combined.

Date shakes are an iconic food of Southern California's Coachella Valley, where the treat originated when date gardens began offering locals and travelers milkshakes made with dates and ice cream.

Recipes courtesy of the **California Date Administrative Committee**.

Slamming Graham Cracker PB&J Nachos

Reproduced with kind permission of **Unilever** PLC and group companies.

Makes: 2 servings
Preparation time: 5 minutes

INGREDIENTS
8 graham cracker squares
¹/₄ cup Skippy® Natural Creamy or Super Chunk Peanut Butter Spread, melted
¹/₄ cup warm reduced sugar grape jelly or strawberry spread
¹/₂ cup chopped apples, bananas, raisins, and/or nuts

METHOD
1. Arrange graham crackers on serving plate. Drizzle with melted Skippy® Natural Creamy Peanut Butter Spread and warm jelly, then top with apples.

TIP: Microwave the jelly in a glass measuring cup to quickly heat up.

Autumn Fruit Compote

Sun-Maid's 1921 recipe book featured several similar fruit desserts.

Makes: 8 servings

INGREDIENTS
1 medium orange
1 medium lemon
4 medium sweet apples, peeled, cored, and each cut into 16 wedges
1 (6 or 7-ounce) package Sun-Maid Dried Peaches
¹/₂ cup (about 6 figs) Sun-Maid Calimyrna Figs

¹/₂ cup Sun-Maid Natural Raisins or Sun-Maid Tart Cherries
¹/₂ cup sugar
1 cinnamon stick
3 cups water
Plain low-fat or Greek-style yogurt (optional)

METHOD
1. Remove the bright colored zest from the orange and lemon, using a vegetable peeler to make wide strips. Squeeze 2 tablespoons juice from the lemon.
2. Combine zest, lemon juice, apples, dried fruit, sugar, cinnamon stick, and 3 cups water in a large saucepan. Bring to a boil, reduce heat, cover, and simmer 15 to 20 minutes, until apples are tender. Cool. Refrigerate in a non-metallic container at least 4 hours to blend flavors.
3. Serve chilled or at room temperature, topped with yogurt if desired.

White Chip Apricot Oatmeal Cookies

HERSHEY'S and HERSHEY'S SPECIAL DARK are registered trademarks. Recipe courtesy of the Hershey Kitchens, and reprinted with permission of **The Hershey Company**.
© The Hershey Company.

Makes: about 3½ dozen cookies

INGREDIENTS:
¾ cup (1½ sticks) butter or margarine, softened
½ cup granulated sugar
½ cup packed light brown sugar
2 eggs
1 cup all-purpose flour
1 teaspoon baking soda
2½ cups rolled oats
2 cups (12-ounce package) HERSHEY'S Premier White Chips
1 cup chopped dried apricots

METHOD
1. Heat oven to 375°F.
2. Beat butter, granulated sugar, and brown sugar in a large bowl until fluffy. Add eggs; beat well. Add flour and baking soda; beat until well blended. Stir in oats, white chips, and apricots. Loosely form rounded teaspoons of batter into balls; place on ungreased cookie sheet.
3. Bake 7 to 9 minutes or just until lightly browned. Do not overbake. Cool slightly; remove from cookie sheet to wire rack. Cool completely.

Date Macaroons

When **"The Settlement" Cook Book** was first published in 1903, recipes were written with assumptions about what cooks knew, so instructions were somewhat vague. Here is an adaptation of the recipe using modern equipment and our tested directions for bake time and temperature.

Makes: about 4 dozen macaroons

INGREDIENTS
1 (8-ounce) package Sun-Maid chopped dates
8 ounces slivered almonds
2 egg whites
$\frac{1}{2}$ cup granulated sugar

METHOD
1. Preheat oven to 350°F. Grease or line baking sheets with parchment paper.
2. Place dates and almonds in a food processor. Pulse about 10 times until dates and nuts are finely chopped.
3. Beat egg whites in a large bowl with an electric mixer until foamy, about 1 minute. Gradually add sugar and beat on high speed until very thick and soft peaks form, about 4 minutes.
4. Fold dates and almonds into egg whites. Drop 2 tablespoon size mounds 2 inches apart on prepared baking sheet.
5. Bake until golden brown and set, 20 to 25 minutes. Let cool 10 minutes on baking sheet; remove with a metal spatula and cool on a wire rack. Cookies will be crisp then soften upon storage. Store in an airtight container.

The first printing of **"The Settlement" Cook Book** was originally entitled **The Way to a Man's Heart** and was published by the Milwaukee Settlement House in 1903. Reprinted with permission from Applewood Books.

Vanishing Oatmeal Raisin Cookies

Recipe reprinted with the permission of **Quaker Oats Company.**

Makes: 4 dozen cookies

INGREDIENTS
$^1/_2$ cup (1 stick) plus
   6 tablespoons butter,
   softened
$^3/_4$ cup firmly packed brown
   sugar
$^1/_2$ cup granulated sugar
2 eggs
1 teaspoon vanilla
$1^1/_2$ cups all-purpose flour
1 teaspoon baking soda
1 teaspoon ground cinnamon
$^1/_2$ teaspoon salt (optional)
3 cups Quaker® Oats
   (quick or old fashioned,
   uncooked)
1 cup raisins

METHOD
1. Heat oven to 350°F. In large bowl, beat butter and sugars on medium speed of electric mixer until creamy. Add eggs and vanilla; beat well. Add combined flour, baking soda, cinnamon, and salt; mix well. Add oats and raisins; mix well.
2. Drop dough by rounded tablespoonfuls onto ungreased cookie sheets.
3. Bake 8 to 10 minutes or until light golden brown. Cool 1 minute on cookie sheets; remove to wire rack. Cool completely. Store tightly covered.

VARIATIONS:
1. Bar Cookies—Press dough onto bottom of ungreased 13 x 9-inch baking pan. Bake 30 to 35 minutes or until light golden brown. Cool completely in pan on wire rack. Cut into bars. Store tightly covered. Makes 24 bars.
2. Other Variations—Stir in 1 cup chopped nuts. Substitute 1 cup semisweet chocolate chips or candy-coated chocolate pieces for raisins; omit cinnamon. Substitute 1 cup diced dried mixed fruit.

Linda's Persimmon Drop Cookies

Makes: about 3 dozen cookies

INGREDIENTS
$^1/_2$ cup butter or
   shortening
1 cup sugar
1 cup persimmon pulp
1 egg
1 teaspoon baking soda
2 cups flour
$^1/_2$ teaspoon each
   cinnamon, cloves,
   and salt
1 cup Sun-Maid raisins
1 cup chopped walnuts

METHOD
1. Heat oven to 350°F.
2. Beat butter and sugar in a large bowl until creamy.
3. Add persimmon pulp, egg, and baking soda; beat until smooth.
4. Stir in flour, cinnamon, cloves, and salt.
5. Mix in raisins and walnuts.
6. Drop rounded tablespoonfuls onto greased or parchment lined baking sheets.
7. Bake until set and bottoms are golden brown, 12 to 15 minutes. Transfer cookies to a wire rack to cool.

Presidential Fruit Cookies

The Lincoln family regularly purchased macaroon pyramids, cookies piled high and held together with spun or caramelized sugar. President Abraham Lincoln also enjoyed fruit, so along with macaroons, he kept his cupboard stocked with fruit cookies.

Makes: 4 dozen cookies

INGREDIENTS
1¹/₂ cups sugar
1 cup soft butter (2 sticks)
3 well-beaten eggs
1¹/₂ tablespoons water
3¹/₄ cups flour
1 teaspoon baking soda
¹/₄ teaspoon salt
¹/₂ teaspoon cinnamon
¹/₂ cup currants
¹/₂ cup raisins, chopped
1 cup walnuts, chopped

METHOD
1. Preheat oven to 350°F.
2. In a large bowl, combine sugar with butter. Cream until fluffy.
3. Add eggs and water and beat thoroughly.
4. In another bowl, sift flour, soda, salt, and cinnamon.
5. Combine dry ingredients with butter and sugar mixture.
6. Add fruits and nuts and mix well.
7. Drop by teaspoon on a greased cookie sheet.
8. Bake for 15 minutes.
9. Remove to a rack to cool.

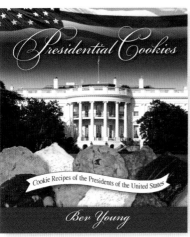

From **Presidential Cookies**; Presidential Publishing 2005, reprinted with permission from the publisher.

Classic Raisin Carrot Cake & Tropical Carrot Cake

From 1992 Sun-Maid
recipe book.

Makes: 12 servings

INGREDIENTS
CAKE
4 large eggs
2 cups granulated sugar
1 cup vegetable oil
1 teaspoon vanilla extract
2¹/₂ cups all-purpose flour
1 tablespoon ground cinnamon
1 teaspoon baking soda
¹/₂ teaspoon salt
2¹/₂ cups finely grated carrots
1¹/₂ cups Sun-Maid Natural Raisins
1 cup chopped walnuts, optional

CREAM CHEESE FROSTING
8 ounces cream cheese, softened
2 tablespoons butter, softened
1 cup powdered sugar
1 teaspoon vanilla extract
2 to 3 teaspoons milk

METHOD
1. Heat oven to 350°F. Coat 10-inch tube pan or 12-cup fluted tube pan with nonstick cooking spray.
2. Combine eggs, sugar, oil, and vanilla in large mixing bowl.
3. Beat with electric mixer until light and fluffy.
4. Combine flour, cinnamon, baking soda, and salt in separate bowl. Gradually add to oil mixture; mix well. Stir in carrots, raisins, and walnuts. Pour batter into greased pan.
5. Bake for 1 hour or until toothpick inserted in center comes out clean. Cool 10 minutes. Remove from pan and cool on wire rack.
6. Combine all frosting ingredients; blend until smooth.
7. Frost top of cake.

VARIATION: **Tropical Carrot Cake**—Reduce oil to ¾ cup and reduce cinnamon to 1 teaspoon. Use golden raisins, if desired. Add one 8-ounce can crushed pineapple, drained; 1 cup sweetened, shredded coconut; ½ cup finely chopped crystallized ginger or 1½ teaspoons dry ginger; substitute ¾ cup chopped macadamia nuts for walnuts. For glaze, increase milk to 2 to 3 tablespoons and blend with frosting ingredients. Drizzle over cake. Garnish with toasted coconut and chopped crystallized ginger, if desired.

Dorothy's Apricot Strudel

Sun-Maid's 1931 recipe book featured baked desserts similar to this treasured family recipe.

Makes: four 12 x 4-inch strudels, about 48 slices

INGREDIENTS
PASTRY
2 cups all-purpose flour
¹/₂ cup butter, softened
1 cup sour cream

FILLING
1¹/₂ cups chopped Sun-Maid Dried Apricots
1 cup apricot jam
1 cup shredded sweetened coconut
1 cup chopped walnuts
Juice of 1 lemon
Powdered sugar

METHOD
1. In a large bowl, stir together flour, butter, and sour cream to make a soft dough. (Or blend in a mixer with paddle attachment). Wrap dough in plastic and refrigerate until well-chilled, 4 hours or overnight.

2. Preheat oven to 350°F.

3. Combine apricots, jam, coconut, walnuts, and lemon juice in a saucepan. Place over low heat and stir just until jam is melted and mixture is blended. Remove from heat.

4. Divide dough equally into four pieces. On a floured surface, roll one piece to an 8 x 12-inch rectangle. Spread one-fourth of the filling in a 3 x 12-inch strip on center of dough. Fold sides of dough over filling; invert onto a baking sheet and tuck ends under. Repeat with remaining dough and filling.

5. Bake until golden brown, 30 to 35 minutes. Cool. Sprinkle with powdered sugar. Slice into 1-inch wide strips to serve.

6. Store whole strudels in an airtight container for up to 3 days or freeze for longer storage.

Quick Peaches & Golden Raisins Cobbler

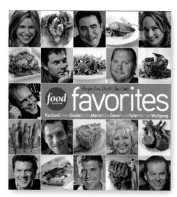

From **Food Network Favorites: Recipes from Our All-Star Chefs**; Wiley 2005; reprinted with permission from the publisher.

Makes: 4 servings

INGREDIENTS

5 to 6 cups frozen sliced peaches (1 large sack)
1 (8-ounce) package complete biscuit mix (recommended: Jiffy™ brand)
$^1/_2$ cup water
$^1/_2$ cup plus 2 tablespoons granulated sugar
2 teaspoons ground cinnamon
$^1/_4$ teaspoon ground nutmeg—eyeball it
$^1/_2$ teaspoon allspice
$^1/_8$ teaspoon black pepper, a couple of pinches
Pinch salt
2 (1-ounce) boxes golden raisins, about $^1/_3$ cup or a couple of handfuls
1 (2-ounce) package sliced almonds, about $^1/_4$ cup
Ice cream or whipped cream for serving (optional)

METHOD

1. Preheat the oven to 425°F. Place the frozen peaches in an 8 x 8-inch glass baking dish and defrost in the microwave on high for about 3 minutes.

2. While the peaches are defrosting, make the cobbler topping: In a bowl, combine the biscuit mix with water. Stir until thoroughly combined but do not overwork. In another bowl, combine the ½ cup sugar, 1 teaspoon of the cinnamon, the nutmeg, allspice, black pepper, salt, and raisins.

3. Remove the peaches from the microwave and combine with the sugar mixture in the baking dish. Top the seasoned peaches with the wet biscuit mix, using your fingers to press it out until even. Top the biscuit mix with almonds. Mix the remaining 1 teaspoon cinnamon and 2 tablespoons sugar together and sprinkle over the top. Bake until the cobbler top is firm and lightly golden and the peaches are bubbly and hot, about 20 to 25 minutes.

4. Serve warm as is or with ice cream and whipped cream if you have some on hand.

La Lechera Apple Raisin Cake

Recipe courtesy of **Nestlé**. All trademarks are owned by Société des Produits Nestlé S.A., Vevey, Switzerland.

Makes: 16 servings
Preparation time: 15 minutes
Cooking time: 35 minutes

INGREDIENTS
6 apples, cored, and sliced
$^3/_4$ cup chopped walnuts
$^1/_2$ cup granulated sugar
$^1/_2$ cup raisins
2 teaspoons ground cinnamon
1 (14-ounce) can Nestlé
　La Lechera Sweetened
　Condensed Milk
1 cup all-purpose flour
$^1/_4$ cup ($^1/_2$ stick) butter, melted
2 large eggs
1 tablespoon baking powder
Powdered sugar
Vanilla ice cream

METHOD
1. Preheat oven to 375°F. Grease 13 x 9-inch baking dish.
2. Combine apples, nuts, granulated sugar, raisins, and cinnamon in large bowl.
3. Pour into prepared baking dish; set aside.
4. Place sweetened condensed milk, flour, butter, eggs, and baking powder in blender; cover. Blend until smooth. Pour batter over apple mixture.
5. Bake for 35 to 40 minutes or until knife inserted in the middle comes out clean. Serve warm sprinkled with powdered sugar and with a scoop of vanilla ice cream.

TIP: This fragrant cake is also wonderful drizzled with Abuelita syrup.

Mexican Rice Pudding

Makes: about 4 cups

INGREDIENTS
1 cup medium or long rice
1 cinnamon stick
1 tablespoon lemon,
　orange, or lime zest
Pinch of salt
4 cups milk
$^1/_4$ cup granulated sugar
$^1/_2$ cup Sun-Maid
　Natural Raisins
1 tablespoon vanilla extract
Ground cinnamon

METHOD
1. Combine 1 cup water, rice, cinnamon, zest, and salt in a deep saucepan with lid. Bring to a boil over medium heat. Reduce heat, cover, and simmer 2 to 3 minutes until water is absorbed.
2. Stir milk and sugar into rice. Simmer over medium-low heat, stirring constantly until rice is soft and milk is thickened and creamy, about 20 minutes, depending on type of rice.
3. Stir in raisins and vanilla. Cook 2 minutes. Remove from heat and let cool 30 minutes (pudding will thicken). Spoon into dessert bowls. Serve warm or chilled sprinkled with cinnamon if desired.

Light Citrus Cheesecake

Makes: 12 servings

INGREDIENTS

CRUST
1 cup Sun-Maid
  Golden Raisins
1 cup walnuts

FILLING
³/₄ cup orange juice
1 envelope unflavored gelatin
³/₄ cup sugar
2 (8-ounce) packages fat-free cream
  cheese, softened
1 (6-ounce) container low-fat lemon
  or orange-flavored yogurt
1 teaspoon grated lemon or orange
  peel
¹/₂ cup Sun-Maid Golden Raisins
Finely shredded or zested lemon or
  orange peel for garnish

METHOD

1. Heat oven to 375°F. Spray a 9-inch springform pan with cooking spray.
2. Process 1 cup golden raisins and walnuts in food processor until finely chopped, about 30 seconds.
3. Press in bottom and ½ inch up sides of springform pan.
4. Bake 8 minutes or until nuts are toasted and crust is set. Cool completely.
5. Combine ¼ cup of the orange juice and the gelatin in 1-quart saucepan. Let stand 5 minutes or until soft.
6. Heat gelatin mixture over low heat just until gelatin is dissolved.
7. Stir in remaining orange juice and sugar. Heat just until mixture is warm and sugar is dissolved.
8. Beat cream cheese in large bowl with electric mixer on medium until light and fluffy. Gradually beat in warm orange juice mixture until well mixed. Beat in yogurt and 1 teaspoon orange peel. Stir in ½ cup golden raisins.
9. Pour mixture into crust. Garnish with citrus peel.
10. Refrigerate at least 2 hours or until set.

Date and Blue Cheese Crostini

A simple combination of dates and mild blue cheese make a rich taste. Broil on crisp crostini and serve warm, or serve cold as a spread for crackers or sliced baguette.

Makes: 24 servings

INGREDIENTS

³/₄ cup Sun-Maid Chopped
  Dates
5 to 6 ounces soft or triple
  cream blue cheese (such
  as Cambazola cheese)
¹/₃ cup finely chopped and
  toasted pistachios or
  pecans
Plain baguette toasts or
  melba crackers
Whole pistachios or pecans
  for garnish

METHOD

1. Chop dates into approximately ¼-inch pieces. Cut rind from cheese.
2. Combine dates and cheese using a fork or flexible spatula until mixture is well blended.
3. Mix in chopped pecans.
4. Spread 1 to 2 teaspoons of date-cheese mixture onto baguette toasts and top with a whole pecan.
5. Place on a baking sheet.
6. Broil 3 to 4 inches from heat, just until bubbly, 1 to 2 minutes. Serve warm.

Turkey Empanadas

Makes: 18 servings
Preparation Time: 20 minutes
Cooking Time: 21 minutes

INGREDIENTS
1 (17.3-ounce) package puff
   pastry sheets, thawed
1 tablespoon vegetable oil
1 medium onion, chopped
2 cloves garlic, chopped
2 cups cooked, shredded turkey
   or chicken
1 (4-ounce) can diced green
   chiles
½ cup water
½ cup raisins
1 tablespoon Maggi Granulated
   Chicken Flavor Bouillon
1 teaspoon ground cumin
1 large egg, lightly beaten

METHOD
1. Preheat oven to 400°F.

2. Heat oil in large skillet. Cook onion and garlic, stirring occasionally, for 3 minutes or until tender. Add turkey, chiles, water, raisins, bouillon, and cumin. Cook, stirring occasionally, for 3 minutes or until heated through.

3. Unfold pastry on lightly floured surface. Roll each pastry sheet into 12-inch square and cut each into nine 4-inch squares (you will have 18 squares total).

4. Place 2 rounded tablespoons turkey mixture in center of each square. Brush edges with beaten egg. Fold squares over filling to form triangles. Crimp edges to seal. Place on baking sheet. Brush with beaten egg.

5. Bake for 15 minutes or until golden. Serve warm or at room temperature.

Good Food, Good Life

Recipe courtesy of **Nestlé.** All trademarks are owned by Société des Produits Nestle S.A., Vevey, Switzerland.

Caramelized Onion, Fig, and Stilton Pizza

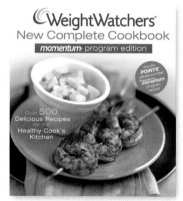

From **Weight Watchers New Complete Cookbook**; Wiley 2009; reprinted with permission from the publisher.

Sweet, large, juicy Vidalia onions, which hail from Georgia, are perfect for caramelizing. If you can't find them, substitute 6 regular yellow onions or 3 yellow and 3 red onions. In this recipe, the natural sugar from the figs also helps to sweeten and caramelize the onions. Savory, tangy Stilton is our first choice of blue cheese here, but you can substitute any good blue-vein cheese, such as Roquefort or Gorgonzola.

Makes: 6 servings

INGREDIENTS
2 teaspoons olive oil
1 teaspoon butter
3 Vidalia onions, thinly sliced
6 dried figs, stems removed, then sliced
1 (10-ounce) thin prebaked pizza crust
3 ounces Stilton cheese, crumbled

METHOD
1. To caramelize the onions, in a 12-inch non-stick skillet over medium heat, heat the oil and butter. Add the onions and cook, stirring occasionally, until light golden, about 6 minutes. Reduce the heat to low, stir in the figs, and cook, stirring occasionally, until the onions are golden brown and well softened and the figs are softened, about 12 minutes.
2. Preheat the oven to 450°F. Place the pizza crust on a nonstick pizza pan or baking sheet. Spoon the onion mixture on the crust, then sprinkle with the cheese. Bake until heated through and the cheese melts slightly, about 15 minutes.

Snappy Salsa

Sweet and spicy, with just the right amount of heat, our favorite salsa can be made with raisins, apricots, or peaches. From appetizers to entrees, quesadillas to grilled fish, it's the perfect addition to your spring meals.

Makes: 3 cups

INGREDIENTS

$^1/_2$ cup diced red bell pepper
$^1/_2$ cup yellow bell pepper
$^1/_2$ cup green bell pepper
1 cup Sun-Maid Natural Raisins or
    Sun-Maid Dried Apricots or Peaches
1 cup diced fresh pineapple
$^1/_2$ cup diced red onion
$^1/_2$ cup diced jicama (optional)
$^1/_4$ cup finely chopped cilantro or parsley
$^1/_2$ jalapeno, seeded and minced
2 to 3 tablespoons lime juice
1 small clove minced garlic
$^1/_2$ teaspoon chili powder
$^1/_4$ teaspoon ground cumin
$^1/_4$ teaspoon salt

METHOD

1. Combine all ingredients in a medium bowl.

2. Cover and refrigerate for at least 1 hour for flavor to develop.

3. Serve with chips, as a dip, on bruschetta (see below), or as suggested above.

BRUSCHETTA: A favorite Italian appetizer and snack. Rub thin slices of baguette (small French bread) with one clove garlic. Grill or bake slices in 350°F oven until crisp, 5 to 10 minutes. Top each slice with 1 tablespoon goat cheese or other soft white cheese and 1 tablespoon Snappy Salsa.

From 1996 Sun-Maid recipe book.

Curried Nut Mix

Recipe courtesy of **Guittard Chocolate Company**.

Makes: 4 cups

INGREDIENTS

$1^1/_2$ tablespoons sugar
4 teaspoons curry powder (hot or mild to your taste)
1 teaspoon salt
2 tablespoons egg whites
2 cups roasted pistachios
1 cup roasted sunflower seeds
1 cup golden raisins
$^1/_4$ cup diced candied or crystallized ginger
1 cup Guittard Real Milk Chocolate Chips

METHOD

1. Preheat oven to 350°F. In a medium bowl combine sugar, curry, and salt. Mix in egg whites. Add nuts and mix well until evenly coated. Spread onto baking sheet lined with *silpat* or foil coated with cooking spray.

2. Bake for about 10 minutes, turning mixture over once or twice to assure even roasting, until surface is dry.

3. Remove from oven and mix in raisins and ginger while still hot. Set on rack to cool completely. Mix in milk chocolate chips. Store in airtight container.

Caribbean Pork Loin with Pineapple Raisin Relish

Originally published in the April 2010 issue of **Better Homes and Gardens® Magazine**. © 2010 Meredith Corporation. All rights reserved.

Makes: 8 servings
Preparation time: 45 minutes
Cooking time: 1 hour 15 minutes

INGREDIENTS

PORK

1 cup packed fresh oregano leaves
1 cup packed fresh cilantro leaves
1/2 cup pineapple juice
1 tablespoons finely shredded lime peel
3 tablespoons lime juice
2 teaspoons kosher salt
4 cloves garlic
1 1/2 teaspoons ground cumin
1/2 cup olive oil
1 (4-pound) bone-in loin center rib roast

RELISH

1 1/2 cups chopped pineapple
1 cup golden raisins
4 green onions, chopped
1/4 cup pineapple juice
3 tablespoons lime juice
2 tablespoons chopped fresh cilantro
1/4 teaspoon kosher salt
3/4 cup canola oil
16 (6-inch) corn tortillas, quartered
2 limes, quartered

METHOD

1. Preheat oven to 325°F. In food processor or blender combine oregano, 1 cup cilantro, 1/2 cup pineapple juice, the lime peel, 3 tablespoons lime juice, 2 teaspoons kosher salt, the garlic, and cumin. Cover and blend or process until chopped. With the motor running, add the olive oil in a thin, steady stream until incorporated.

2. With sharp knife, score surface of pork roast with small slits. Place roast in roasting pan, bone side down. Pour herb mixture over roast. Roast, uncovered 1 1/4 to 1 3/4 hours or until an instant-read thermometer inserted into center of roast reads 150°F, spooning herb mixture over meat two or three times during roasting. Lightly tent with foil and let stand 10 minutes. Temperature will rise to 160°F.

3. For relish, in bowl combine pineapple, golden raisins, green onions, 1/4 cup pineapple juice, 3 tablespoons lime juice, 2 tablespoons cilantro, and 1/4 teaspoon kosher salt.

4. In large skillet, heat canola oil over medium heat. Cook tortilla wedges in hot oil for 15 to 20 seconds per side. Drain on paper towels. Wrap in foil to keep warm.

5. To serve, cut meat from bone and thinly slice. Serve with tortilla wedges, relish, and garnish with lime wedges.

Quick Chicken Curry

Makes: 3-4 servings

INGREDIENTS

3/4 pound boneless, skinless
   chicken breasts, cut into
   1/2-inch pieces
3 tablespoons vegetable oil, divided
1 small red bell pepper, cut into
   1/2-inch pieces
1/4 cup minced onion
1 tablespoon all-purpose flour
1 tablespoon curry powder
1 1/2 cups Pearl® Organic Soymilk
   Creamy Vanilla
3/4 teaspoon salt
Hot cooked rice
Condiments: cashews, raisins,
   toasted coconut

KIKKOMAN®

Recipe courtesy of **Kikkomanusa.com**

METHOD

1. Stir-fry chicken in 1 tablespoon hot oil in wok or large skillet over medium-high heat 2 minutes. Add bell pepper and stir-fry 2 minutes longer; remove.

2. Reduce heat to medium-low; heat remaining 2 tablespoons oil in same pan. Add onion; stir-fry 2 minutes.

3. Stir in flour and curry powder; cook 1 minute. Gradually stir in soymilk and salt. Bring to boil, stirring constantly.

4. Add chicken mixture; cook and stir until heated through.

5. Serve over rice and top with condiments.

Chicken and Asparagus with Raisin-Wine au Jus

A wonderful dish that's the perfect star for a spring lunch or dinner.

Makes: 4 servings

INGREDIENTS
2 tablespoons finest olive oil
4 Foster Farms Boneless Skinless Chicken Breasts
Salt and pepper
2 tablespoons butter
1½ tablespoons finely minced garlic
1 pound fresh asparagus, trimmed and cut into 2-inch pieces
¼ cup raisins
¼ cup hearty red wine, such as cabernet or pinot noir

METHOD
1. In a large skillet or sauté pan, heat olive oil over medium heat until warmed. Add boneless skinless chicken breasts and cook for approximately 7 minutes, or until golden brown on all sides.
2. Season with salt and pepper to taste, remove from pan and keep warm.
3. Drain any excess liquid from pan and warm two tablespoons of butter over medium heat.
4. Sauté the finely minced garlic for 2 minutes. Add the asparagus, cover, and cook for 2½ minutes.
5. Add the red wine and the raisins, and continue cooking until the wine has evaporated.
6. Pour over cooked chicken breasts and serve.

Recipe courtesy of
Foster Farms.

Cranberry-Raisin Turkey Wraps

From 2005 Sun-Maid recipe book.

Makes: 6 servings

INGREDIENTS
½ cup water
½ cup brown sugar, packed
⅓ cup sugar
¼ cup cider vinegar
2 cups fresh or frozen cranberries
¾ cup Sun-Maid Natural Raisins
½ cup chopped onion
1 tablespoon fresh ginger, grated
½ teaspoon red pepper flakes
6 tablespoons cream cheese, softened
1½ cup shredded sharp cheddar cheese
6 (8-inch) flour tortillas
1¼ pounds sliced deli turkey
6 tablespoons chopped walnuts
½ cup fresh cilantro, chopped

METHOD
1. Combine water, sugars, and vinegar in a medium saucepan over medium heat. Stir until sugars dissolve.
2. Add cranberries, raisins, onion, ginger, and pepper flakes. Bring to a simmer and cook 5 to 10 minutes or until slightly thickened. Cool. Cover and refrigerate until chilled.
3. Preheat oven to 350°F. Mix together cream cheese and cheddar cheese; spread about 3 tablespoons on each tortilla. Top with several slices of turkey, 2 to 3 tablespoons cranberry-raisin mixture, 1 tablespoon walnuts, and one heaping teaspoon of cilantro.
4. Roll up tortillas and wrap individually in aluminum foil. Place on a baking sheet and bake 5 to 10 minutes until heated through. Serve warm.

Moroccan Garbanzo Beans with Raisins

Garbanzo, chickpea, ceci: this bean with many names shares culinary history with Mediterranean, Middle Eastern, Indian, and Mexican cultures. Unlike most cooked legumes, this nutty-flavored bean has a firm texture.

Recipe courtesy of
BettyCrocker.com

Makes: 4 servings
Preparation time: 20 minutes
Total time: 20 minutes

INGREDIENTS

1¹/₃ **cups uncooked regular long-grain white rice**
2²/₃ **cups water**
1 tablespoon peanut or vegetable oil
1 large onion, sliced
1 medium onion, chopped (¹/₂ cup)
1 clove garlic, finely chopped
1 cup diced acorn or butternut squash
¹/₄ **cup raisins**
1 cup vegetable broth
1 teaspoon ground turmeric
1 teaspoon ground cinnamon
¹/₂ **teaspoon ground ginger**
1 (15 to 16-ounce) can garbanzo beans, drained, rinsed

METHOD

1. Cook rice in water as directed on package.

2. Meanwhile, in 3-quart saucepan, heat oil over medium heat. Add sliced onion, chopped onion, and garlic; cook about 7 minutes, stirring occasionally, until onions are tender. Stir in remaining ingredients except garbanzo beans.

3. Heat to boiling. Reduce heat; cover and simmer about 8 minutes, stirring occasionally, until squash is tender. Stir in beans; heat thoroughly. Serve over rice.

Make the most of this recipe with tips from
The Betty Crocker® Kitchens.

Fresno-Valley Zucchini and Raisins Pizza

Makes: 4 servings

INGREDIENTS

1 tablespoon olive oil
1 large clove garlic, minced or pressed
1 teaspoon grated lemon zest
1 small zucchini
1 large or 2 small Valley Lahvosh round flat bread
$^1/_2$ cup (4 ounces) crumbled feta cheese or soft goat cheese
$^1/_3$ cup Sun-Maid Natural Raisins
$^1/_4$ cup shredded Parmesan cheese
1 tablespoon pine nuts

METHOD

1. Preheat oven to 375°F.

2. Combine olive oil, garlic, and lemon zest in a medium bowl.

3. Slide a vegetable peeler firmly along the length of the zucchini to make thin "ribbons." Mix zucchini ribbons thoroughly with olive oil mixture.

4. Crumble feta or spread goat cheese evenly over lahvosh.

5. Sprinkle raisins over cheese. Arrange zucchini evenly on top, lightly folding and mounding zucchini ribbons. Sprinkle with Parmesan and pine nuts.

6. Bake on oven rack or a baking sheet for 10 minutes or until cheese is melted.

Lemon and Date Chicken Salad

Dates and cinnamon are a sweet contrast to tangy lemon and green onion in this pleasantly different chicken salad.

Makes: 4 servings

INGREDIENTS

2 tablespoons lemon juice
2 tablespoons olive oil
2 tablespoons sliced green onions
1 tablespoon fresh, chopped cilantro or parsley
$^1/_2$ teaspoon ground cinnamon
$^1/_4$ teaspoon salt
$2^1/_2$ cups diced or shredded cooked chicken
$^1/_2$ cup Sun-Maid Chopped Dates
$^1/_3$ cup thinly sliced celery
$^1/_3$ cup coarsely chopped, toasted cashews or peanuts (optional)

METHOD

1. Combine lemon juice, olive oil, green onion, cilantro or parsley, cinnamon, and salt in a medium bowl.

2. Stir in chicken, dates, celery, and cashews.

3. Cover and refrigerate 1 hour before serving to blend flavors.

4. Serve as an entrée salad, in a tortilla wrap, in a sandwich, or as a pocket bread filling.

Chicken with Olives and Dates

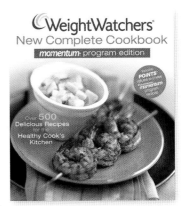

From **Weight Watchers New Complete Cookbook**; Wiley 2009; reprinted with permission from the publisher.

This Middle Eastern-inspired dish combines sweet spices, fruit, and poultry with olives. You might like to try it on a bed of couscous.

Makes: 4 servings

INGREDIENTS
1 tablespoon olive oil
2 garlic cloves, crushed
1 teaspoon minced peeled fresh ginger
1 teaspoon ground cumin
$^1/_2$ teaspoon paprika
$^1/_4$ teaspoon turmeric
$^1/_4$ teaspoon cinnamon
$^1/_4$ teaspoon salt
1 pound skinless boneless chicken drumsticks
$^1/_4$ cup low-sodium chicken broth
$^1/_4$ cup dried apricot halves, chopped
2 pitted dates, coarsely chopped
10 small kalamata olives, pitted and chopped
1 tablespoon grated lemon zest
1 tablespoon water

METHOD
1. To prepare the marinade, in a gallon-size zip-close plastic bag, combine the oil, garlic, ginger, cumin, paprika, turmeric, cinnamon, and salt. Add the chicken. Seal the bag, squeezing out the air; turn to coat the chicken. Refrigerate, turning once, for 1 hour. Drain and discard the marinade.
2. Spray a large nonstick skillet with nonstick spray, and heat. Add the chicken and broth; cook, covered, for 15 minutes. Turn the chicken over; sprinkle with the apricots, dates, olives, lemon zest, and water. Cook, covered, checking occasionally, until the chicken is cooked through, about 15 minutes longer. If the chicken begins to stick to the skillet, add 1 to 2 tablespoons more water.

Raisin Serrano Quesadillas

Makes: 4 servings

INGREDIENTS
10 (3 to 4 ounces) Serrano peppers
1 teaspoon olive oil
2 tablespoons regular or reduced sodium soy sauce
$\frac{1}{2}$ cup Sun-Maid Natural Raisins
4 (8 to 10-inch) flour tortillas
8 ounces shredded Monterey Jack cheese
Sour cream
Cilantro for garnish

METHOD
1. Slice Serrano peppers lengthwise in half. Remove stems and seeds. Thinly slice into lengthwise strips. (Wear gloves to protect hands.)

2. Heat olive oil in a small frying pan. Add pepper strips and cook over medium heat 3 to 4 minutes, stirring constantly until peppers begin to blister and soften. Add soy sauce and raisins. Cook 30 seconds or until liquid is nearly evaporated. Remove from heat and set aside. (Be sure to work in a well-vented area.)

3. Heat a wide frying pan over medium heat. Brown one side of one tortilla; flip tortilla over and place one fourth of the cheese and peppers on half the tortilla. Fold the other half of the tortilla over the filling. Continue to cook over medium heat, turning once to brown the other side. Repeat with remaining tortillas.

4. Cut in wedges and serve with sour cream and cilantro.

Spicy Asian Slaw

Makes: 4 servings

INGREDIENTS

3 tablespoons rice vinegar
2 tablespoons soy sauce
1 tablespoon dark sesame oil
$^1/_4$ teaspoon crushed red pepper flakes
4 cups (8 ounces) packaged coleslaw mix
   (shredded fresh cabbage and carrots)
$^1/_2$ cup Sun-Maid Natural Raisins
$^1/_3$ cup thinly sliced green onions
$^1/_4$ cup peanuts or chopped cashews (optional)

METHOD

1. Combine vinegar, soy sauce, sesame oil, and pepper flakes. Mix well.

2. Add coleslaw mix, raisins, and green onions. Toss well.

3. Chill at least 1 hour or up to 24 hours before serving. Sprinkle with peanuts, if desired.

Recipes for Spicy Asian Slaw and Broccoli Pasta Toss are from the 2002 Sun-Maid recipe book.

Broccoli Pasta Toss

Makes: 4 servings

INGREDIENTS

MAIN DISH
1 cup small broccoli florets
1$^1/_4$ cups cooked shell pasta
$^1/_2$ cup Sun-Maid Natural
   Raisins
$^1/_3$ cup chopped red onion
$^1/_4$ cup chopped red bell
   pepper

DRESSING
$^1/_3$ cup reduced-
   calorie
   mayonnaise
1 tablespoon cider
   vinegar
$^1/_2$ teaspoon sugar
Salt and pepper

METHOD

1. Combine all salad ingredients.

2. Combine all dressing ingredients and blend well.

3. Pour dressing over salad. Add salt and pepper to taste. Toss and serve.

Dolmas Salad

After making dolmas—stuffed grape leaves shown at right—one chef did not want to discard the grape leaf pieces left over. So she combined them with other dolma ingredients into a salad. It would make a wonderful side dish for roasted lamb. Preserved grape leaves are sold in jars in Middle Eastern markets and in many well-stocked supermarkets.

Makes: 4 to 6 servings

Recipe courtesy of
Sunset Magazine.

INGREDIENTS
$^1/_4$ **cup pine nuts (1 ounce)**
$^1/_2$ **cup thinly sliced green onions (white
     and pale green parts only)**
1 tablespoon olive oil
1$^1/_2$ cups long-grain white rice
**2$^1/_2$ cups fat-skimmed chicken broth or
     vegetable broth**
$^1/_2$ **cup chopped preserved grape leaves
     (reserve $^1/_4$ cup brine)**
$^1/_4$ **cup lemon juice**
$^1/_4$ **cup raisins**
$^1/_4$ **teaspoon pepper**
$^1/_4$ **cup chopped parsley**
$^1/_4$ **cup chopped fresh dill**
1 lemon (optional), rinsed and quartered

METHOD
1. In a 4- to 6-quart pan over medium heat, stir pine nuts and ¼ cup green onions in oil until nuts begin to brown and onions are limp, about 5 minutes.

2. Stir in rice, chicken broth, grape leaves and reserved ¼ cup brine, lemon juice, raisins, and pepper. Bring to a boil, then reduce heat to low, cover, and simmer until liquid is absorbed and rice is tender to bite, 30 to 35 minutes.

3. Fluff rice mixture with a fork; stir in parsley, dill, and remaining ¼ cup green onions. Mound salad on a platter and garnish with lemon quarters if desired. Serve warm or at room temperature.

Albacore Waldorf Salad

Makes: 2 servings
Preparation time: 10 minutes

INGREDIENTS

1 (2.6-ounce) pouch or
   1 (5-ounce) can StarKist®
   Albacore Tuna in Water
1 tablespoon lemon juice
2 tablespoons raisins
$^1\!/_4$ cup mayonnaise
$^1\!/_8$ teaspoon ground cinnamon
1 large size apple, cored, and
   chopped
$^1\!/_2$ cup chopped celery
2 tablespoons walnuts or
   pecans, chopped
2 tablespoons milk
Sugar, to taste

METHOD

1. In a large bowl, toss together apples and lemon juice.
2. Add celery, raisins, walnuts, and tuna. Toss gently.
3. In a medium bowl, combine mayonnaise, milk, and cinnamon. Blend well. (For a sweeter dressing, add sugar.)
4. Pour dressing over apple-tuna mixture. Toss gently to coat.

TIP: For a lower-fat version, use reduced fat or nonfat mayonnaise and nonfat milk.

Raisin Carrot Salad

Makes: 6 servings

INGREDIENTS

$1^1\!/_2$ cups grated carrots
1 cup Sun-Maid Natural
   Raisins
$^1\!/_2$ cup thinly sliced celery
$^1\!/_2$ cup chopped walnuts
   (optional)
$^1\!/_3$ cup low-fat mayonnaise
   or plain yogurt

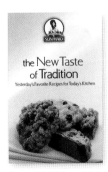

From 2007 Sun-Maid recipe book.

METHOD

1. Combine all ingredients and toss well.
2. Cover and refrigerate until chilled.

SERVING SUGGESTION: **Sandwich**—Serve raisin carrot salad in pocket bread or tortilla roll-up with smoked deli turkey.

Moroccan Quinoa

Recipe courtesy of **Nestlé.**
All trademarks are owned by
Société des Produits Nestlé S.A.,
Vevey, Switzerland.

Perfect for any night of the week,
this Moroccan-inspired dish
features a flavor-rich combination
of quinoa, cilantro, pine nuts, and
dried fruit. Serve as a side dish
or add cooked meat or fish for a
meal all its own.

Makes: 6 servings, ½ cup each
Preparation Time: 10 minutes
Cooking Time: 20 minutes
Cooling Time: 5 minutes standing

INGREDIENTS
1 tablespoon extra-virgin olive oil
½ cup chopped shallots
1 large clove garlic, finely chopped
1 cup water
1 cup Apple Nestlé Juicy Juice® All Natural 100% Juice
1 cup ivory quinoa, rinsed
1½ teaspoons Maggi Granulated Chicken Flavor Bouillon
½ teaspoon ground cumin
⅓ cup currants or chopped dried cherries or cranberries
⅓ cup coarsely chopped fresh cilantro
¼ cup pine nuts, toasted
Ground black pepper

METHOD
1. Heat oil in medium saucepan over medium-high heat. Add shallots and garlic; cook, stirring occasionally, for 2 minutes or until fragrant.
2. Stir in water, Juicy Juice, quinoa, bouillon, and cumin. Bring to a boil; reduce heat to medium-low. Cover; cook for 15 minutes or until most of liquid is absorbed.
3. Remove from heat; stir in currants. Cover; let stand for 5 minutes.
4. Add cilantro and pine nuts; fluff with fork and serve. Season with pepper.

Apple-Raisin Stuffing

Recipe courtesy of
Campbell Soup Company.

Makes: 6 to 8 servings

INGREDIENTS
$^1/_4$ cup ($^1/_2$ stick) butter
1 stalk celery, chopped (about $^1/_2$ cup)
1 small onion, chopped (about $^1/_4$ cup)
1 (10$^1/_2$-ounce) can Campbell's® Condensed Chicken Broth
4 cups Pepperidge Farm® Herb Seasoned Stuffing
1 medium apple, cored, and chopped (about 1 cup)
$^1/_4$ cup raisins
$^1/_4$ teaspoon ground cinnamon

METHOD
1. Heat the butter in a 10-inch skillet over medium heat. Add the celery and onion and cook until tender, stirring occasionally. Add the broth and heat to a boil. Remove the skillet from the heat. Add the stuffing, apples, raisins, and cinnamon and mix lightly. Spoon the stuffing mixture into a 1½-quart casserole.

2. Bake at 350°F for 25 minutes or until the stuffing is hot.

Lentil Cakes

Recipe courtesy of the **Produce for Better Health Foundation** (PBH). Find this recipe and others like it online at www.FruitsAndVeggiesMoreMatters.org.

Makes: 8 servings
Preparation time: 1 hour 15 minutes

INGREDIENTS

3 curry leaves or ½ teaspoon of curry powder
1 cup crimson lentils
1 cup beluga lentils
1 cup split peas
1 cup sweet onions, diced
1 tablespoon garlic, minced
1 tablespoon olive oil
3 quarts water
2 tablespoons garam masala
3 tablespoons olive oil, to sauté the cakes
⅓ cup raisins
¼ teaspoon salt or to taste
¼ teaspoon black pepper or to taste

METHOD

1. Pour olive oil into a large saucepan over medium heat and sauté the onions and garlic until translucent. Add lentils, split peas, garam masala, and curry, and sauté for about 3 to 5 minutes. Add water to the mixture and bring it to a gentle boil. Bring heat down to a simmer and cook until soft, then drain cooking liquid.

2. In a food processor, puree three quarters of the mixture until nice and smooth, saving one quarter for texture.

3. Fold whole lentils and raisins into puree and mix well. Adjust seasoning if necessary.

4. Portion into 2 to 3 ounce cakes. Sauté over medium heat and sear lentil cakes one minute per side. Serve immediately with your favorite chutney or salad.

Grilled Baby Eggplant With Raisins, Pine Nuts, and Rosemary

fitness
Mind, Body + Spirit

Recipe courtesy of
Fitness Magazine.

Makes: 5 servings
Preparation time: 10 minutes
Cooking time: 15 minutes

INGREDIENTS
½ cup goat cheese
1 tablespoon finely chopped
   rosemary
½ cup extra-virgin olive oil
2 tablespoons balsamic vinegar
½ teaspoon salt plus additional for
   seasoning
6 baby eggplants (about 2 pounds),
   trimmed and halved lengthwise
Freshly ground black pepper
3 tablespoons raisins
3 tablespoons pine nuts

METHOD
1. In a bowl, combine the goat cheese and rosemary. Cover tightly with plastic wrap and refrigerate until ready to use. In a separate bowl, whisk together the oil, vinegar, and ½ teaspoon of salt.
2. Preheat a grill to medium-high heat. Brush the eggplant with the marinade and season with salt and the black pepper to taste. Reserve remaining marinade.
3. Transfer the eggplant to the grill cut side down. Close cover and cook, 5 to 7 minutes, turning once halfway through, until eggplant is very tender and lightly charred.
4. Remove eggplant from grill and spread the cut side of each half with goat cheese mixture. Top each half with a sprinkling of raisins and pine nuts. Return eggplant to grill cut side up. Close cover and cook until goat cheese is slightly melted, about 30 seconds. Drizzle with reserved marinade and serve.

Index

A

Adams, Ansel 61
advertising 58-63, 128
airplanes 130
alcohol 87
animated Sun-Maid Girl 17, 51, 61, 68-9
apples 22, 29, 115
 apple raisin cake 155
 baked apples with granola 144
apricots 22, 28, 39, 106-7
 apricot strudel 153
 white chip apricot oatmeal cookies 148
Arabic, dried fruit references 35
Armenian growers 92
Aristotle 36
Australia 123
Austria 125

B

barbecue sauce 19
bakeries 128
Bear brand 58
Berg, E.A. 7, 10
Berlin Airlift 12, 124
beta-carotene 118
Bible, dried fruit references 34
biscuits, cinnamon-raisin 141
Blossom Trail 115
blueberries 116
Blue's Clues 65
Blue Ribbon Peaches 114
bonnet, Sun-Maid 15, 55
boron 118-9
brandy 87
bread, raisin 128-9
 prize raisin bread 134

C

California Associated Raisin Company 10, 11, 52, 54-59
California Raisin Advisory Board 13, 15, 61
California Raisin Marketing Board 16
Calimyrna figs 110-111
calorie needs, daily 31
Canada 26, 97, 120
cantaloupe 117
carrot cake 24, 152
 tropical carrot cake 152
cereal 18
cheesecake, light citrus 156
cherries 116
chicken: chicken and asparagus with raisin-wine au jus 162
 chicken with olives and dates 165
 quick chicken curry 161
Children's Day 26
China 24, 121, 126, 135
Chinese Lunar New Year 24
chocolate covered raisins 16, 18
chocolate covered fruits 23
Church, Moses 44
climate 43, 77
cobbler, peaches and golden raisins 154
coleslaw 20
 spicy asian slaw 167
colony farm system 42
compote, autumn fruit 147
consumer stories 70-3
cooperatives 10, 52
corn flour raisin cake 135
cranberries 116
 cranberry-raisin turkey wraps 162
crostini, date and blue cheese 156
cultivation of grapes, first 34
currants 102-3
Czech Republic 125

D

dates 23, 112-113
date shakes 113, 146
Dancing Raisins 15, 61
dehydrators 104-5
Denmark 122, 124
dental health 119
distillery, Sun-Maid 87
Diwali 27
dried-on-the-vine harvesting 84-5
doll, Sun-Maid collectible 16
DOVine grape variety 41, 102, 104

E

Easter 24
Easterby, Anthony Y. 44
eggplant, grilled 173
Eisen, Francis T. 38
empanadas, turkey 157
Eriksson, Leif 36
equivalency, fresh/dried 28-9, 41

F

Fiesta grape variety 41, 102-4
fiber, dietary 118-9
figs 23, 29, 110-1
Fig Newtons 111
Finland 124
five a day programs 41
Flame Seedless grape variety 103
Forkner, J.C. 111
food chart, United States 31, 122
food guidelines, international 120-2
French toast, banana 143
Fresno Scraper 44
Fresno Station 39
fruitcake 22, 125
fruit cookies, presidential 151
frost 14, 88

G

garbanzo beans with raisins, Moroccan 163
Germany 98, 121, 125
Gold Rush 42
golden raisins 91, 104-5
Gooseberry Patch 17
granola 18, 142
granola bars 20
grapevines, planting 76-7
growing grapes 78-9, 88
growing areas: San Joaquin Valley 40

Sacramento Valley 40
Santa Clara Valley 39, 107
Guinness Book of Records 15

H

Harding, Warren G. 11
harvesting raisins: hand harvesting 80-81
 mechanical harvesting 82-3
 dried-on-the-vine harvesting 84-5
harvesting plums 109
headquarters, Sun-Maid 50-1, 90-1
holidays, fruit and food 25
horse-drawn plow 130
hot cross buns 24, 140

I

immigration, California 42, 92-3
India 121, 126, 136
Indonesia 126-7
international flags 98-9
international food guidelines 120-2
irrigation 44-5

J

Japan 26, 98, 120, 126-7, 129, 135
Japanese growers 92
Jefferson, Thomas 37
Jewish cookery 25, 125

K

Kearney, Martin Theodore 42, 52
Keeler, William N. 7
King, Anita 58
Korea 121

L

Lent 24
lentil cakes 172
Lincoln, Abraham 151
logos, Sun-Maid 11, 13, 14, 50, 59

Acknowledgments

Sun-Maid would like to thank the following for their kind permission to reproduce their images:

(Key: a-above; b-below/bottom; c-center; f-far; l-left; r-right; t-top)

The Fresno Morning Republican: 10tc, 47tr, 57tl, 58cl. **Fresno Bee:** 13tl, 13bl, 15br, 16tc. **iStockphoto.com:** Viktar Malyshchyts 14tr (plums), 28bl, 108tc, 117tc; Jack Puccio 18bl; LVV 18bc; Joe Potato Photo 18br, 21tr; bettina sampl 19tl; Shawn Gearhart 19tr, 19br; Joe Biafore 20tl, 27c, 116br; JoKMedia 20tr; Norman Pogson 20cr; Ethan Myerson 20bl; AdShooter 20br; William Mahar 21 tl; Lauri Patterson 22tr, 125ftc; WEKWEK 24tr; Carly Hennigan 25tl; Sarah Bossert 25tr; Alex Slobodkin 25b (calendar); akiyoko 26tr; Kyu Oh 26cl; Amelia Johnson 26cr; Kulpreet_Photography 27tl; Nikhil Gangavane 27tr; foodandwinephotography 27b; Joachim Angeltun 28tc (scale); Matej Michelizza 28tl (peach), 29 fbl, 114c; BEZERGHEANU Mircea 29cl (figs), 111cl; Mark Herreid 30tl; Rick Hoffart 30tc; diane39 30tr; Steven Wynn 31br; Michael Flippo 42bl; Don Bayley 51tr; Fedor Patrakov 87cr; Lya_Cattel 92tr, 115cr; dandanian 98c (clock); Kent Steffens 99tc; melhi 99tr; Lulu Durand 109bc; Elzbieta Sekowska 109br; cynoclub 110b; Jill Fromer 111bl; Paul Cowan 112cl; Dean Turner 115bfl; Sarah Lee 116tl; Dimitris Stephanides 116c (dried cranberries); YinYang 116tr; eli_asenova 116c (cherries); kalimf 116bc; Alina Solovyova-Vincent 116cr (dried blueberries); Tim Abramowitz 117cl; Yong Hian Lim 117tr; tropicalpix 117bl; Andrjuss Soldatovs 117bc; Daniel Bendjy 117cr (papaya); Elena Schweitzer 117fbr; Matthew Jones 118tr; Volodymyr Krasyuk 119tl; Nataliia Fedori 119ftr (clouds); Gustavo Andrade 119cr; Iuliya Sunagatova 119cl; Ruslan Ivantsov 119br (salt); Talaj 119bl; Magdalena Kucova 125 ftr, 125tr; Antonio Ribeiro 125tc; MorePixels 125c; Andrea Skjold 126cl; Elena Semenova 127bl; Stephen Strathdee 130cr; dblight 130bl; lisegagne 130bc; Tim Boryer 130br; Orlando Rosu 131tr; oversnap 139tr; Roman Ivaschenko 150br; zkruger 171r. **Simon & Schuster, Inc.:** 16c. **The Reader's Digest Association, Inc.:** 17bc, 65 tr. **Facebook:** 17tr. **Maybeck Foundation:** 17br, 57 br. **General Mills Inc.:** 21bfl. **Post Foods, LLC:** 21bl. **Attune Foods:** 21bc. **Quaker Oats Company:** 21br. **Kellogg Company:** 21bfr. **StockFood:** Bender–StockFood Munich 23tl. **Fotolia:** web2000ra 28cl (apricots), 106br; Secret Side 29tl (apple), 115tl; nito 116fbl (dried cherries); Daryl Musser 117fbl (dried pineapple); Carmen Steiner 125cr; ExQuisine 125bl; JJAVA 127tr. **PhotoDisc Inc.:** 29ftl. **United States Department of Agriculture:** 31tr, 122tl, 122tr. **Alamy Images:** Robert Harding Picture Library Ltd 34tr; The Art Gallery Collection 35tl; North Wind Picture Archives 36l. **Bridgeman:** *Still Life of Flowers and Dried Fruit*, 1611 (oil on panel) by Clara Peeters (1594-1659) Prado, Madrid, Spain/ Giraudon/The Bridgeman Art Library 37tr. **Corbis:** Araldo de Luca 35tr; Alfredo Dagli Orti/The Art Archive 36r. **Dorling Kindersley:** Neil Lukas 17cr, 57bl; Alistair Duncan 34b; Rob Reichenfield 37cr; Demetrio Carrasco 37bl; Angus Osborn 37br; Steve Gorton 42tl; Roger Phillips 46tl; Dorling Kindersley 69tr (film strip); Ian OLeary 107tl. **Wikimedia Commons:** Amadalvarez 35cr. **California Date Administrative Committee:** 35br, 112b, 113tl, 113cl, 113bl, 113tc, 146. **Proceedings of the Massachusetts Historical Society,** v. 51: 37cl. **Joaquin Sorolla y Bastida:** 38tr. **Fresno County Public Library, California History and Genealogy Room:** 38bl, 39cr, 44t, 45bl, 45bc, 45br, 47tl, 109cl, 111br. **California Dried Plum Board:** 39tl, 108b, 109tl, 109tr. **Apricot Producers of California:** 39cl, 106tr, 106bl, 107cl, 107c, 107cr. **Canadian Produce Marketing Association** (Fruits and Veggies—Mix it up!): 41tl. **5 A DAY @ NSF-CMi Ltd.:** 41cl. **Produce for Better Health Foundation** (Fruits & Veggies—More Matters): 41 c, 172. **International Nut and Dried Fruit Council Foundation:** 41bl. **Informa UK Ltd.** (FoodNews): 41bc. **Edwin M. Eaton,** *Vintage Fresno* (Fresno: The Huntington Press, 1965): 42tr. **California State Library,** California History Section, Sacramento: 42cl. **M. Theo. Kearney,** *Fresno County, California, and the Evolution of the Fruit Vale Estate,* revised ed., Fresno, 1903: 43tl. **The Interior,** v.1, no. 4 (Fresno: December 1895): 44br. **Charles C. Colby,** *The California Raisin Industry–A Study in Geographic Interpretation,* Annals of the Association of American Geographers v. 14, no. 2: 45t. **Vincent Petrucci** and **Malcolm Media Press:** 46r, 87tr, 103, 119tr. **Gustav Eisen,** *The Raisin Industry* (San Francisco: H.S. Crocker, 1890): 46br. **Pop Laval Foundation:** 47c, 96r, 111tr, 114br, 130tr. **M. Rieder,** Los Angeles, circa 1910: 52br. **Western Novelty Co.,** Los Angeles: 53bl, 114tr. **The San Francisco Bulletin:** 55tl. **SanFranciscoMemories.com:** 56tr. **Ansel Adams Publishing Rights Trust:** 61bl. **Norman Rockwell Museum:** 62tl, 62br. **E.C. Publications, Inc.** (Mad Magazine): 64r. **Sesame Workshop** (Sesame Street): 64l. **FOX** (The Simpsons): 65c. **Viacom International Inc.** (Blue's Clues): 65b. **Hasbro** (Monopoly): 65tl. **Penguin Group:** 72br. **Midland Tractor:** 82b. **SFI Inc.:** 87trb. **Charles Weidner,** San Francisco, circa 1910: 92c. **Jon Marthedal:** 93tr. **Kane is Able, Inc.:** 97cl, 97bl. **Valley Fig Growers:** 111tl. **Edward Mitchell,** San Francisco, circa 1915: 111bc. **Fresno County Blossom Trail:** 115cl. **Health Canada:** 120tr. **Ministry of Health, Labour and Welfare** (Japan): 120b. **German Nutrition Society:** 121tl. **Chinese Nutrition Society:** 121tr. **Korean Nutrition Society:** 121bl. **National Institute of Nutrition** (India): 121br. **Ministry of Food, Agriculture and Fisheries** (Denmark): 122bl. **National Food Agency** (Sweden): 122br. **Secretary of Health** (Mexico): 123tl. **Department of Health and Ageing** (Australia): 123tr. **Food Standards Agency** (United Kingdom): 123br. **Ministry of Health** (Turkey): 123bl. **Bauducco Foods:** 129cl, 129c, 129cr, 129bl, 129br. **RAC Japan:** 135tl, 135tr. **Betty's Kitchen Magazine:** 135bl, 135br. **Meredith Corporation:** 131 cl, 142r, 160l, 160r. **Wiley:** 136tr, 141br, 144, 154, 158tr, 165tr. **King Arthur Flour Company:** 138. **Unilever PLC and group companies:** 147tl, 147tr. **The Hershey Company:** 148tr. **Applewood Books:** 149br. **Presidential Publishing:** 151br. **Société des Produits Nestlé S.A.:** 155tl, 155tc, 157, 170l, 170r. **Guittard Chocolate Company:** 159bc. **KikkomanUSA.com:** 161cr. **Foster Farms:** 162cr. **BettyCrocker.com:** 163cr. **Valley Lahvosh Baking Co.:** 164tr. **Starkist Co.:** 169tl, 169cl. **Campbell Soup Company:** 171l. **Fitness Magazine:** 173.

Special thanks to Jerry Winters, cover design. Cover art © Sun-Maid Growers of California